To Sharlet,

I'm happy that our paths in life have crossed

Arlene
5/95

By Arlene Taylor

BACK TO BASICS
Timely Tips for Building Bona Fide Boundaries
& Optimum Self-Esteem

WHOLE BRAIN SUCCESS STRATEGIES
Identifying & Maximizing Innate Giftedness

GENDER GRAPHICS
Understanding & Appreciating
Male/Female Differences

THRESHOLDS TO THRIVING

A Power Pack of Practical Rx's

Arlene Taylor PhD
Lorna Lawrence PhD
Illustrations by Debby Wilmot

Realizations Inc
Napa California

THRESHOLDS TO THRIVING

Editors:
    Leona Glidden Running PhD
    Edward Cherney
Cover illustration:
    Debby Wilmot
Computer assistance/research data input:
    Michael Johnson

Typestyle: Times New Roman
First printing 1995

Library of Congress Catalog Card Number: 95-68491

ISBN 1-887307-97-4 $12.00 Softcover

Published by:

Realizations Inc
Success Resources International
P.O. Box 2554 Napa CA
94558-0255

TABLE OF CONTENTS

INTRODUCTION

The inspiration for this book was triggered by comments voiced in counseling sessions and in seminars presented internationally. Comments such as: "I was not affirmed as a child;" "I never learned how to affirm myself;" "How can I learn to affirm myself and others?"

According to the dictionary, the word *affirm* means to validate, to state positively. Practically, this indicates a nurturing communication style; one in which we talk to ourselves and to others in a positive manner. It has been said that by the time we reach adulthood, most of us have heard between seven and nine negative comments for every positive. Is it any wonder that we don't know how to practice the art of affirmation successfully?

Many of us were not taught how to affirm ourselves or others because our parents had not learned from their parents, and so forth. In order to successfully validate and encourage others, we must begin with ourselves. With concerted effort we can learn to confidently talk to ourselves in a positive communication style; we can incorporate affirmations into our lives on a daily basis; we can learn to pass along this gift to others.

Do we really need to use affirmations? Absolutely. Human beings need encouragement. The consistent use of affirmations is a practical way in which to encourage oneself and others. There are many ways in which to develop this habit. We recognize that various individuals use different terminology and definitions. Therefore, we encourage you to bring what you have already learned with you into this process. Develop the affirmations habit in the style that best suits you and your individuality—so that it truly becomes part of you.

Other concerns voiced pertained to developmental task completion: "I feel like the only person struggling with boundary development;" "I wonder if others have problems with trust;" "Are my problems today connected to events that happened to me in the past?" We believe there definitely is a connection between the events of childhood and behaviors exhibited in adulthood. Accordingly, we designed a research project that would provide us with information about the perceived connection between problems in adulthood and incompleted developmental tasks of childhood. Selecting twenty-four pertinent tasks, we created a survey instrument and recruited volunteers. They were reached by acquaintances, by mail, and at seminar presentations. Two hundred and thirty-two women responded; one hundred and three men. The participants may represent a more motivated segment of the population. Nevertheless, they do embody a composite sampling from several national backgrounds including the United States, Canada, and Australia.

The purpose of The Developmental Task Survey was to determine individual participant's perception of the presence and frequency of problems in adulthood that may be connected to a lack of successful completion of one or more of twenty-four significant developmental tasks of childhood. Participant responses are included throughout. The last line of each table—labeled **Me**— is left blank for reader input. Refer to Research data for demographic information.

We offer heartfelt thanks to those who asked the questions that motivated us to begin our research and to the hundreds of survey participants who willingly shared their perceptions. We also thank our *mentors* who have helped us to realize the power of affirmations and who have encouraged us in our personal growth journey.

We believe that the most practical way in which to express our thanks is to pass along to others that which we have found so practical. This book is an endeavor to do just that. It is divided into twenty-four chapters with each chapter defining a developmental task. We believe the successful completion of each task contributes to our ability to become actualized (made real through action), differentiated (autonomously interdependent), productive adults. This list of twenty-four tasks is neither exhaustive nor absolute—it is a practical beginning. We gratefully acknowledge the work of Erik Erikson in this area.

Although most of us have the ability to learn to live affirmingly without formal therapy or counseling, in order to accurately identify the scope of needed improvements we must specifically and systematically evaluate our lives. The interwoven exercises and research components can assist you in this process.

The *practical prescriptions* are both efficacious and fun. Overall, this book is designed to increase your awareness (the first step on the continuum of positive change), to stimulate your thinking, and to direct your attention to new options that can enhance your life and help you to thrive. It is not designed to take the place of professional care and the authors do not take responsibility for the improper application of concepts presented herein. Every effort has been made to present these concepts as clearly and with as much accuracy as possible. Terminology and meanings do vary, however, and may be interpreted differently by different individuals.

As you study the definitions and vignettes, as you answer the questions for yourself, and as you complete the exercises, you may identify personal problems in one or more of these developmental task arenas. We encourage you to discuss these with your significant other, best friend, counselor, therapist or support group. True recovery requires healthy interaction with others.

Finally, affirmation is eminently compatible with belief in a Higher Power. Human beings seem to possess an innate desire to connect with and/or to worship a Being that is more powerful than themselves—a desire that appears to be unrelated to race, ethnicity, culture, or geographic location, although behaviors exhibited often differ dramatically. In this sense, affirmations can be viewed as *spiritual* inasmuch as they can enable us to relate more nurturingly to ourselves, to others, and to a Higher Power. For individuals connected with a twelve-step program, we believe learning to nurture and affirm the self can contribute significantly to recovery from addictive behaviors.

In this growth process, we encourage you to be generous when reinforcing your progress. Give yourself feedback and affirmation. Continually picture the person you are becoming. Modify your learning techniques to match your needs. Above all, practice, practice, practice.

Bon Voyage!

—The authors

STUDY SUGGESTIONS

For many of us, effective study habits have receded into the dim dark past—if they ever existed. Because the idea of *study* may initially prove intimidating, we offer a few guidelines. Principles of adult education suggest that learning is more effective when:

- **The material to be learned is related to what the learner already knows.** Use the information in this book to build on what you already know. For example, you may have already completed portions of a developmental task and simply need to continue the growth process. Or you may already possess intellectual knowledge and simply need to transform it into consistently applied skills.

- **The learner is an active participant and not just a passive recipient of others' knowledge.** You will get out of this book what you put into it. Set aside the time to complete the written exercises and to create affirmations that apply directly to you personally.

- **The information is integrated with practical problem-solving.** As you learn, ask yourself how the information can be applied specifically to a problem in your life. Be open to looking at problems as well as solutions in a new way. Theoretical information often remains just that, theoretical—unless we take action and implement it on a daily basis.

The overall goal is to be able to recall the information and to apply it in a practical manner. In general, we tend to remember:

- 10% of what we read
- 20% of what we hear
- 30% of what we see
- 50% of what we both see and hear
- 80% of what we say
- 90% of what we act upon.

Because of this, we suggest that you read the information aloud. This will enable you to <u>hear</u> what you <u>see</u>. Write the affirmations down, paraphrased to fit you. Repeat them aloud. Talk to yourself about the information you are learning and the skills you are developing. And finally, take action based upon what you see, read, write, and hear. As you gradually incorporate the information into your daily life you will come to *own* it.

Studies have shown that when we consistently repeat a behavior for **twenty-one days**, we are well on our way to developing a *habit*. When you identify a developmental task that needs more attention than another, you may want to spend at least three weeks concentrating on that topic. For example, on day one, read aloud our definition of the developmental task. Continue for the next nine days, contemplating the sample affirmations and completing the exercises. For energizing emphasis, take another ten days to review the whole program. On the twenty-first day, revise your personal affirmation for that developmental task as needed and transfer it to a card. Carry it with you and/or attach to your bathroom mirror. Spend as much time on each task as you need and then go on to another.

Since the 90s have been declared *the decade of the brain*, it is appropriate to include a few practical applications derived from recent research. Briefly, the largest portion of the human brain is known as the cerebrum. It is composed of the left and right hemispheres and divided by natural fissures into four portions or quadrants. Each quadrant possesses innate abilities that can help us to develop specific skills or competencies—although there may be some overlap because the brain is so complex and adaptable (refer to the diagram at the end of Study Suggestions).

Brain researchers (notably Benziger and Sohn) believe that the majority of human beings are born with a preference for using one or two of the cerebral quadrants over the others, a tendency known as *brain lead*. This means that some skills are more easily acquired while the development of others requires more time and energy.

Here are examples of some of the functions believed to be directed by each quadrant:

- The frontal left cerebral quadrant, composed of the left frontal lobe, helps us to set and achieve goals. By breaking down the information in this book into twenty-four segments and by further dividing each segment into ten *bites,* we have tried to give you a head start on developing manageable goals. This quadrant can help us to prioritize the steps in this learning process and to make decisions about *how, when, where,* and *why* the information will be incorporated into our individual lives. The frontal left helps us to stay on track and provides us with the mental energy necessary to manage willpower appropriately. Use the functions of this quadrant to set goals for learning to affirm yourself and others and to complete development tasks as necessary.

- The lower left cerebral quadrant is composed of the left temporal, occipital, and parietal lobes. This portion of the brain helps us to organize our activities and to follow the routines necessary to include the use of affirmations on a consistent basis. The lower left quadrant enables us to repeat our desired routines accurately. However, we must make a concerted effort each day to do so. Use the functions of this quadrant to schedule time each day to practice the art of affirming yourself and others.

- The lower right cerebral quadrant is composed of the right temporal, occipital, and parietal lobes. It helps us to create harmony and to stay in touch with ourselves and others. The successful completion of the developmental tasks and the creation of an affirming lifestyle can help to promote harmony in your life. You can connect with others without violating your own boundaries or theirs and thus avoid potential conflict in many cases. Use this quadrant to help you learn to love yourself and others unconditionally, to sing your affirmations (it is believed to be the home of innate musical ability), to give yourself permission to make mistakes in the learning process, and to tap into a Higher Power for assistance.

- The frontal right cerebral quadrant, composed of the right frontal lobe, helps us to see the big picture and to move toward creating positive change in our individual lives. The twenty-four line drawings can help us to actively picture each developmental task and to practically apply the concept in a variety of situations. This quadrant enables us to generate new ideas for exhibiting functional behaviors that can enhance personal growth. It can help you to compose a new melody, to "set your affirmations to music," or to write affirmations in poetic form. Use the functions of this quadrant to create positive internal pictures and to rehearse seeing yourself successfully exhibiting appropriate behaviors on a regular basis. Remember that the ancestor of every behavior is a thought. Visualizing an internal picture is one way of thinking.

The quadrants were designed to work together. Consequently, we can be most effective when we allow each to contribute its specialty. By calling on the innate strengths of all four cerebral quadrants, you can be successful in completing these and other developmental tasks and in creating an affirming lifestyle. In addition, you will be able to role-model high-level-wellness living to others and may even become the *change-agent* to break the cycle of dysfunction in your lineage. When we identify a weakness (lack of developed skills) in one or more quadrants, we can decide to develop the needed skills and/or we can team up with another individual who has strengths in our area of weakness. Yes, others can contribute to our ability to function in a whole-brain manner even as we help them to do likewise.

The two right-brain quadrants particularly enjoy information presented through stories. Consequently, we have included incidents from the lives of real people; names have been changed to preserve confidentiality.

Each line-drawing contains a reminder of our need to learn to *watch over* ourselves. For some of us, this is a developmental task in and of itself!

A WHOLE-BRAIN APPROACH

© Arlene Taylor PhD

THE CEREBRUM

Frontal left quadrant	Frontal right quadrant
✓ Prioritizing ✓ Managing willpower ✓ Setting and achieving goals	✎ Visualizing ✎ Grasping the *big picture* ✎ Inspiring innovative change

← Central Fissure →

Lower left quadrant	Lower right quadrant
■ Organizing ■ Following routines accurately ■ Maintaining the status quo	☺ Harmonizing ☺ Connecting (others, Higher Power) ☺ Pursuing personal growth

↑

Longitudinal Fissure

TRUST

CHAPTER ONE
SPOTLIGHTING TRUST

Trust—Day One

Synonyms: Assurance, belief, certainty, confidence

Antonym: Mistrust

The power of *faith* is a developmental task that ideally is learned during the first year of life. Developing the ability to trust appropriately enables us to establish confidence in the self, in others, in a Higher Power, and in life overall. Webster's offers several synonyms for the adjective *appropriate,* including: proper, suitable, becoming, fit, and apt. This indicates that the type of trust we need to develop is based on some type of evidence and is congruent with the circumstances involved. In other words, there are times in life when it is healthier and safer not to trust in a specific instance, just as there are times when it most beneficial to do so.

If we fail to develop appropriate levels of trust, as adults we may exhibit a lack of confidence in everyone and everything or evidence blind faith in everyone and everything. We may confuse caretaking with caring, intensity with intimacy, control with concern, obsession with dedication. We may misinterpret *security* as a need to be in control of everyone and everything. We may succumb to apathy or total despair.

The youth pastor of a large congregation used a simple but effective object lesson to demonstrate trust to his parishioners. After blindfolding his preschool son, he carefully guided the child to the top of a six-foot step-ladder. When the child stood steadily on the top step, the pastor moved into position in front of the ladder and announced, "I am ready to catch you, son. Are you ready to jump?" Still blindfolded, the boy nodded and jumped confidently into the waiting arms of his father. Blind trust? No way. Confident trust based on solid experience.

Millie's job required a great deal of travel overseas. At first, she dreaded the ordeal and was fearful of going through customs, finding her way through unfamiliar airports and negotiating transportation in foreign countries. She mistrusted her ability to handle these tasks, especially when she was also required to deliver irreplaceable documents. She eventually reduced her dread of travel by learning to trust herself. She said, "Others have done this before me. I can do it, too." And she did.

Some of us did not have earthly parents that role-modeled appropriate levels of trust. In such cases, our inability to trust can pervade all aspects of life. Learning to trust safely and wisely may well be a lifelong task. We can learn to trust ourselves; to establish confidence in our ability to identify and meet our needs. We can learn to have faith that we will always be there for us; that even when we make mistakes (and hopefully learn from them), we can always be our own best friend.

Next we can branch out and learn to have confidence in others. We neither expect them to be perfect, to meet all our needs, nor to take care of us. We can learn to wisely select individuals with whom we can create a mutual support system, one in which we can share affirmation. We can learn to identify our needs and our wants, to recognize the difference between them, and to verbalize them to ourselves and to others. We can trust ourselves to meet our needs and some of our wants. We can also trust individuals within our support system to help us in the process—at least to some degree.

For some of us, a helpful starting-point strategy can be learning to place our confidence and reliance in a Higher Power, a *parent-of-choice*. We can learn to rest our minds, as Webster's puts it, on the integrity, veracity, justice, and trustworthiness of our Higher Power. The Twelve Steps of Alcoholics Anonymous link the concept of a Being greater than ourselves with "God as we understand Him." We acknowledge that there may be as many different labels and interpretations of God or a Higher Power as there are philosophies. Nevertheless, it can be helpful for each of us to define our concept and beliefs about a Higher Power and to put some energy into developing a spiritual relationship with such a Being.

Learning to appropriately trust ourselves, others, and a Higher Power forms the foundation for many of the succeeding developmental tasks. Developing the skill of appropriate trust involves making healthy, functional decisions in at least five areas:

- Whom we will trust. Everyone? Certain individuals?
- Why we will trust. The evidence for or against trusting?
- When we will trust. All the time? Some of the time?
- Where we will trust. Everywhere? Nowhere?
- How we will trust. Completely? Selectively?

Most of us could benefit from evaluating our ability to trust appropriately; some will need to complete this developmental task. Its successful completion can enable us to resolve some problems in adulthood, to avoid some problems altogether, and to heal woundedness. We can then help to support others in their progress.

Sound, serene, secure, safe trust is not built in an instant. It is a little bit like climbing a mountain. We take one step at a time, each one moving us farther along on our journey. We get nowhere until we take the first step, however. For some, this first step may mean simply making the decision to discover the truth about trust. For others it may mean grieving breaches of trust in the past. For still others it may mean taking a risk and believing in themselves and in others. Whatever that first step is for you, take it now and watch the proverbial tiny acorn grow into a strong healthy oak.

Trust—Day Two

Table One—Problems related to trust   Females—219 Males—102

	Never	Rarely	Sometimes	Frequently	Always
Females	13.2%	28.3%	37.5%	16.9%	4.1%
Males	15.7%	25.5%	32.4%	22.5%	3.9%
Overall	14.0%	27.4%	35.8%	18.7%	4.1%
Me					

Take a few moments to evaluate yourself:
- Do I trust everyone—even when past events have shown that this may be unwise?
- Do I not trust anyone, not even my Higher Power?
- Is there a specific problem in my life related to trust?

Trust—Day Three

Our learned behaviors of the past need not be
carried forward into the future "as is." Old Adage

I am making a list of the events in my life that have contributed to my developing an ability to trust appropriately. Likewise I am listing the factors that influenced me to fail to trust. I am looking at these events and factors from a new perspective and I am learning from them. I can keep the positive and gently let go of the negative. I realize that in my own strength, I am powerless to use this information to develop the ability to trust wisely. Today I place my confidence in my Higher Power. I willingly share my disappointments as well as my hopes and dreams. I recognize my need for personal growth because there are problems in my life. The status quo doesn't *cut it* any more. I choose to develop the ability to trust wisely. I am on my way.

Trust—Day Four

I trust the butcher, the baker, and the
candlestick maker; why not myself? Unknown

When I stop to think about it, I do trust others—the dentist, my doctor, the adult-education instructor, the cab driver, my hair dresser, the mechanic. So why not include myself in this list? Today I am learning to trust, wisely and appropriately. I begin by trusting that I have the wisdom and the courage to safely place my confidence in a Higher Power. I see the seeds of trust springing up in my heart and mind and I water them faithfully. I am learning to trust myself and to prove worthy of that trust. It is based on solid experience. I believe that I am developing the ability to trust— therefore I am. I like the feeling of confidence that ensues. I have stopped limiting myself through the use of negative words and self-defeating messages. I choose to reinforce my success with empowering words of validation.

Trust—Day Five

It's not wise to allow yesterday's
failures to bankrupt today's efforts. Unknown

I deal gently with myself as I learn to have confidence in myself. Just because I have not yet learned to trust appropriately does not mean I can never learn to do so. I do have the ability to develop appropriate levels of trust. I am wisely and confidently teaching myself to walk this new pathway of trust. This journey is one of healing. Today my entire soul is lifted up. My strength is renewed as I learn the joy of trust. I recognize some of the defense mechanisms I developed to protect myself during childhood. They helped me then but I no longer need all of them now. I replace the learned barriers of fear and apprehension with a sense of confident joy and trust—in my Higher Power and in myself. Yesterday's mistakes are not ruining my progress today.

Trust—Day Six

I have put my trust in you. Psalm 143:4

I am learning to trust in a Higher Power, learning to believe that a Being outside of myself does care for me. Although there is *silence* at times and although I do not understand every particular, I am experiencing that deeper rest and I am glad. Today I appreciate the changes that I am seeing in my life. I am consistently practicing new patterns of prudent trust. I realize that it will take time to change old undesirable patterns—perhaps a month for every year that I practiced the old behaviors. I am trusting myself to be content with today's growth. I have faith in my ability to learn new patterns of trust. I am able to learn from my mistakes. I can learn a new way to go. Based on past and present evidence I am developing criteria that must be met by those in whom I will place my trust. This is a great way to live!

Trust—Day Seven

*A successful journey consists of many individual steps,
each taken one at a time. Trust is one of those steps. Proverb*

I am carefully listening to the self-talk messages about trust that play inside my head, paying attention to what I hear and evaluating each phrase for its potential to nurture and affirm me or discourage and sabotage. When I recognize negative phrases that reinforce doubt and fear, I make a decision to change them. I may not be able to *erase* all of them completely but I can turn down the volume on those old unhelpful messages. Today I concentrate on creating new positive self-talk messages and recording them on my internal compact disc player. I am rehearsing thoughts that help me to build a sense of appropriate trust, messages that will be replayed continually whether or not I am consciously aware of them. This exercise is helping me to be successful in building trust.

Trust—Day Eight

In God I trust; I will not be afraid. Psalm 56:11

I am learning to trust moment by moment as I walk the journey of life. I realize that it is not enough to simply read what others have said about trust. I need to take that journey myself; to live my life with confidence. I know that tomorrow I will again walk confidently into the future. I have more energy because I am not wasting it through fearful, anxious thoughts and behaviors. I do what I can today and plan for tomorrow. As I heal, I am discovering the gift of laughter. It lightens my heart and makes me happy that I am learning to trust.

Identify one specific behavior, in relation to trust, that you are determined to improve.

_____

_____

Trust—Day Nine

List three things you have learned about yourself and trust.

- _____

_____

- _____

_____

- _____

_____

Trust—Day Ten

Congratulations! Appreciate the progress you have made in learning to trust appropriately. Write down your personal trust affirmation.

_____

_____

_____

_____

_____

_____

_____

HOPE

CHAPTER TWO
ACCENTUATING HOPE

Hope—Day One

Synonyms: Expectancy, anticipation, aspiration, longing

Antonym: Despair

The power of positive *expectation* is a development task that is paired with trust. Learning to hope enables us to develop a sense of secure dependence upon a Higher Power and upon ourselves. Webster's defines the word hope as a desire for some good accompanied with at least a slight expectation of obtaining it or a belief that it is obtainable. Together, trust and hope help us to develop an ongoing sense of delightful anticipation. We look forward to each new day knowing that something good is about to happen—or that we can find the good in every eventuality.

If we did not learn to develop a realistic sense of hope, as adults we may settle for whatever is in the present; fail to expect that anything better is obtainable; or long for unattainable outcomes. An inability to hope appropriately can contribute to our becoming immobile and ineffective; can sabotage our ability to take action on our behalf; can lead to depression.

Unfortunately, many people misunderstand and misuse hope. After reading about Princess Di's marriage, Althea began to hope for a similar relationship. She turned down all dates while waiting for a royal prince. She is still waiting, lonely but hopeful. Because of dynamics within her family-of-origin, she had learned to hope for tooth-fairy cures, miraculous events, and for some force outside of her to bring magic into her life. In order to thrive, Althea will need to reassess the lessons learned during her childhood and make a concerted effort to develop a balanced and realistic sense of hope.

When his wealthy uncle gave Tom a new Corvette as a college graduation gift, Alec began to hope that someone would give him such a present as well. However, when no such gift was forthcoming from Alec's financially-strapped family, he petulantly decided that life was not fair and began to feel depressed. Rather than set realistic goals based on changes that he himself could control, Alec hoped—even fantasized—that others would somehow turn his dreams into reality. His magical thinking had all but immobilized him.

Tom and Althea had learned nonproductive patterns of thinking. As pointed out by Irving, "The same weakness of mind that indulges absurd expectations, produces petulance in disappointment." We must learn to hope *realistically*—as related to both ourselves and others and then learn to take personal responsibility for achieving expected outcomes. This does not mean that we cannot set our sights high. It does mean that we learn how to face facts, to see things as they really are, to be practical, to define our needs versus our wants, and to take personal responsibility for seeing that our needs (and some of our wants) are met.

Helen Keller, although blind, exhibited unwavering *hope.* She believed that when one door of happiness closes another one opens. So often however, we look so long at the closed door that we do not see the one that has opened. *Hope* is what enables us to look for the open door; to expect that there *is* an open door—or at least an open window—even as *trust* enables us to be confident that we will recognize the opening.

Realistic hope teaches us that "with God, all things are possible." As the Navajo saying so succinctly puts it, "There is a way out of every dark mist over a rainbow trail." We can focus on what we can do, to start turning our realistic hopes into actuality. Metaphorically, this may mean that instead of just sitting and waiting for someone to bring us flowers, we need to plant our own garden.

Learning to hope realistically involves making a decision to accept the present and anticipate the best. It has been said that what we receive in life is often not what we deserve but what we *expect.* Choose to be a balanced optimist. Learning to contemplate positive outcomes and putting our energy into working toward them, while always remaining centered in reality, can turn the tide from failure to success. Joyful anticipation does not come to live with us unbidden and uncultivated. We must invite it into our lives on a daily basis.

An unknown writer penned these words:

A crowd of troubles passed him by,
As he with courage waited.
He said, "Where do you troubles fly
When you are thus belated?"

"We go," they said, "to those who mope,
Who look on life dejected,
Who weakly say good-bye to hope.
We go—where we're expected!"

As we did with trust, we will need to make some decisions about hope. For example:

- What we want to hope for. Specific goals? Global goals? Personal goals? Family goals?
- Why we want to hope. To improve our health? To attract prosperity?
- When we will hope. All the time? In adversity? In prosperity? In sickness? In health?
- Where we will hope. Everywhere? At home? At work?
- How we will hope. Consistently? Periodically? Skeptically? Realistically?

Hope—Day Two

Table Two—Problems related to hope   Females—217 Males—102

	Never	Rarely	Sometimes	Frequently	Always
Females	24.4%	29.5%	29.9%	11.1%	5.1%
Males	17.7%	34.3%	23.5%	17.6%	6.9%
Overall	22.3%	31.0%	27.9%	13.2%	5.6%
Me					

Take a few moments to evaluate yourself:

- Do I begin my day with a sense of positive expectation?
- Do I feel hopeless; do I lack enthusiasm?
- Are there problems in my life related to hope?

Hope—Day Three

As for me, I will always have hope. Psalm 71:14

I am making a list of the events in my life that have contributed to my developing an ability to hope realistically. Likewise I am listing the factors that influenced me to hope unrealistically or to fail to hope at all. I am looking at these events and factors from a new perspective and I am learning from them. I can keep the positive and gently let go of the negative. I realize that hope must be a constant in my life, like a thread of gold throughout my day. It enables me to expect that I will succeed in learning to hope. It builds upon the confidence that I have developed. I am evaluating my fondest dreams and realistically setting goals to achieve those dreams.

Hope—Day Four

The parent of faith is hope. Anonymous

I do not deprive myself of hope as often as I have in the past. I may be all I have to hang on to—but I have me. Today, hope gives me the courage to explore and to experience life to the utmost. Hope helps me to trust even as the ability to trust helps me to hope. It musters joy through to the end of my day. Life is becoming more of an adventure and less of a chore. I have realistic dreams and desires and I know that I can achieve them. Hope sings a song of praise that increases joy beyond my fondest dreams. I remind myself, "I am on my way, rejoicing!"

Hope—Day Five

A longing fulfilled is a tree of life. Proverbs 13:12

Hope is my life jacket in rough seas, the rope ladder I hang on to when my life temporarily falls apart. I believe that my Higher Power is supporting me internally no matter what is happening around me. This positive expectation helps to prevent heart sickness and despair; it refreshes me as would a *tree of life.* Today I am role-modeling realistic hope. I am centered on doing the tasks that need to be done in order to start turning my dreams into realities. My life is no longer a collection of hopeless dreams. I am learning that I can control only the changes that are occurring within me. Because of that, my energy is being directed toward making the positive changes that will enable me to realize my goals. I know that those changes are leading me toward success.

Hope—Day Six

Sitting still and wishing is only tempting fate.
God provides the fish but we must dig the bait. Unknown

I dare to hope where others have not. I am less discouraged by the pessimistic responses of others. Alone in my thoughts, I trust my hopes and I can see through the night. I can see tomorrow's dawn. Because of my positive expectations, I know I will succeed even when the going is temporarily rough. Were the seas always calm, I would not see the golden wings of hope. I do not expect some external force to keep the seas of my life calm in all situations. I do expect that the changes within me are teaching me how to keep my internal bastion calm. Today I do not expect success to be handed to me nor do I sit and wait to win the lottery. I expect success and I am willing to work hard. There have been too many times in the past when I was immobilized by fear and helplessness. Not any more! I roll up my sleeves and start digging.

Hope—Day Seven

One who has hope has everything. Arabian proverb

I am truly beginning to enjoy my personal journey. For the first time in my entire life I am experiencing the joy that accompanies growth. I am learning to trust and to hope. I am learning to expect that I have everything I need in order to succeed. I have everything I need in order to be *me,* and to be *me* is to succeed. Today I understand that having *things* is less important than having the real me. I like the person I am becoming. I trust and expect that I am able to provide for the things that I need in life. I have more energy with which to accomplish tasks because I have given up the habits of worry and anxiety. What a drain they were on my energy—how I look forward now to each new day! I evaluate the self-talk tapes about hope that play inside my head. I turn down the volume on old unhelpful messages and concentrate instead on the new positive self-talk messages I am recording. I rehearse thoughts and words that help me to build a sense of positive expectation.

Hope—Day Eight

Hope unswervingly. I Corinthians 13:13 (TM)

My hope is strong. I recognize the opportunities that surround me. I enjoy today, realizing that joy is both a choice and a gift and that I can choose to magnify that gift. I look for even small blessings to celebrate. I know that what happens to me is less important than my response to what happens to me. I expect to feel joy within me and to see joy around me. I look for the *gift*, the lesson I can learn, in every situation. I enjoy the challenges that I meet in this process. I see myself looking very pleased as my dreams are being realized.

Identify at least one specific behavior, in relation to hope, on which you are working.

_____

_____

Hope—Day Nine

List three facts about yourself and hope.

- _____

_____

- _____

_____

- _____

_____

Hope—Day Ten

Bravo! The power of realistic positive expectations is becoming a habit. Write down your personal affirmation of hope.

_____

_____

_____

_____

_____

_____

_____

AUTONOMY

CHAPTER THREE
EMPHASIZING AUTONOMY

Autonomy—Day One

Synonyms: Self-determination, self-governance

Antonym: Enmeshment

The power of personal *identity* is the developmental task that ideally is begun during the second and third years of life and then honed throughout life. Identity enables us to possess a personal sense of who we are as separate and distinct individuals, to see ourselves against the expansive mosaic of humanity. We are able to work through power struggles. We often act very independently but at the same time feel very dependent inwardly. We gradually develop a picture of our strengths and weaknesses, rejoice in our strengths and work to strengthen areas of weakness.

According to the dictionary, the word identity is the condition of being the same as was described or claimed. Personal identity is the ability to know oneself, to be oneself, to describe oneself, and to role-model the self that we claim to be. Authentic autonomy is hand in glove with the concept of *being real.*

If we failed to acquire a functional sense of personal identity, we may experience confusion about who we really are. We may become demoralized, totally lacking nerve, pluck, and personal power. We will be at risk for becoming chameleons, taking on the characteristics of the persons with whom we associate rather than maintaining a sense of our own uniqueness. As adults we will likely vacillate between relationship enmeshment and total isolation. We will likely experience difficulty creating and implementing bona fide boundaries—balanced, healthy, functional personal limits.

We help to build a sense of autonomy by learning to say the word *no,* often inappropriately at first and then more efficaciously and graciously. The so-called terrible twos is really a period in life when we are trying to learn to differentiate and individuate—to develop autonomy. Some of us were not allowed to say no as children, and consequently do not know how to say no appropriately as adults.

During her childhood, Angela had never been permitted to say no. Consequently, she had to develop this skill in adulthood. At first, early in her reparenting journey, she was very tentative and people sometimes disregarded her timid no. She practiced saying no more effectively, alone in front of her mirror at first. She can now laugh as she recalls how the word no barely came out in a tiny whisper. Gradually she learned to increase the volume of her voice so that the word sounded solid and certain. For a time during this process, she even wore a button that read, "What part of no don't you understand?"

Realizing that many other people also have problems with saying no can help us to keep rejection in perspective. A valued friend in her eighties gave us a very helpful hint (one we shared with Angela). This mentor suggested that we memorize what she referred to as the eleventh commandment, "Thou shalt not explain." Indeed, there are often situations in which it is most helpful to simply say a pleasant no or no thank you and let it go at that.

Jim and John were identical twins. As a teenager, John began to assert his autonomy. He first took a stand against always wearing clothing identical to that of his brother. It was a landmark day when he came home from the barber with a different hairstyle. At first, the other members of the family were uncomfortable with these changes. Gradually, however, they learned to respect John's wishes. He, in turn, felt more confident about himself and became a greater achiever as he perceived himself both connected to his twin and yet separate. John discovered a part of himself that had lain dormant and thereby enriched both himself and his family.

As adults we need to learn that we can only truly say yes once we have learned to say no. When we are comfortable with no, then we can develop the skill of knowing when to use it efficaciously. This will help us to become and to maintain who we were intended to be. To overuse or underuse the power of no simply reflects two extremes of a spectrum. In the final analysis, we can only truly connect with others once we have recognized, developed, embraced, and honored our own identity.

Living autonomously requires a delicate and intricate dance between the extremes of independence and dependence. True autonomy represents a state of interdependence, the development of which requires us to make decisions about:

- Isolation versus enmeshment
- Personal boundaries (refer to Showcasing Boundaries)
- Caring versus caretaking (codependency)
- Expectations (ours as well as those of others).

Individually we need to evaluate our position on the continuum of autonomy and strive to become truly interdependent rather than swinging back and forth between the extremes of independence and dependence or hovering at one extreme. To know who we truly are is empowering. From such a position we can ride the waves of plenty, avoid being devastated by adversity, and stand firm amid the winds of strife—knowing that externals cannot destroy our autonomy.

Our core identity may remain constant but as we grow and mature, facets of our identity grow and mature as well. Nick says that one of the reasons he enjoys life so thoroughly is that each day is an adventure, one in which will be revealed some new facet of his emerging identity. May his tribe increase!

Autonomy—Day Two

Table Three—Problems related to autonomy   Females—214 Males—102

	Never	Rarely	Sometimes	Frequently	Always
Females	23.8%	36.5%	19.6%	16.4%	3.7%
Males	26.5%	32.4%	23.5%	12.7%	4.9%
Overall	24.7%	35.1%	20.9%	15.2%	4.1%
Me					

Take a few moments to evaluate yourself:

- Are my thoughts and opinions my own or do they primarily reflect the expectations of others?
- Do I perceive myself as a separate and unique entity?
- Are there problems in my life related to autonomy?

Autonomy—Day Three

What I do when only I am looking is my true ID. Lawrence

I am making a list of the events in my life that have contributed to my developing a personal identity. Likewise I am listing the deleterious factors that caused problems in the sphere of personal autonomy and led me to exhibit dependent or independent behaviors rather than *interdependent* behaviors. One event did not make me who I am, neither will looking at just one event help me to gain the big picture. I am learning to look at these events and factors from a new perspective. Today I choose to retain the positive and willingly let go of the negative. I am making these decisions more easily and more decisively. I understand that in order to gain something new I often have to let go of something old. It is more than a fair exchange. I am not diminished in the process.

Autonomy—Day Four

*Comparing myself to others can cause me to
lose sight of the unique person I am. Anonymous*

I am learning from what has happened to me in the past; I am concentrating on the here and now. Today I rejoice in the moment and discover peace in just being. I refuse to worry about the future because I am confident that I will handle whatever arises. I realize that what lies within me, my individual potential, is more important than anything that happened in the past or anything that will happen in the future. I continue to enjoy the process and do not fear the passage of time because I know that I am lovable at all ages. Many wonderful things in life come in multiples—sunsets, rainbows, roses, stars—but there is only one of me. My uniqueness is a gift I cherish and that I share with the world. Others share their particular uniqueness. Together we are enriched. What an exciting concept!

Autonomy—Day Five

What I think makes all the difference. Anonymous

I am learning to pay attention to what happens within me. I obtain satisfaction from finding out about my inner being. I am getting to know myself. Gradually, I am growing beyond the need to remain a child. I am not waiting for someone else to rescue or fix me. I am capable of taking care of myself and of reparenting myself to maturity. I do not need anyone else's permission to be myself. Today I see who I am at my core, where the *real me lives.* The great redwood trees of the forest stand alone and yet together. I enjoy standing alone in a position of comfortable interdependence. I do not desire to crowd another, so I do not stand too close. I want to be able to easily lend a helping hand and to receive the same, so I do not stand too far away. Knowing who I am allows me to move freely in the social jungle; sometimes closer and sometimes removed—but always comfortable with who I am. I share my uniqueness with others and am inspired and nurtured by theirs. Although our uniqueness is different, one is not better or more valuable than the other.

Autonomy—Day Six

This above all; to thine own self be true. Shakespeare

Today I continue the process of learning who I am. I separate who I am from the person others think I am or ought to be. I strive to present the *real* me to myself and to others. It is exciting to be true to myself. I drop the *mask* that has shrouded me for so long and I risk letting the world see the real me. I respect the person I am. This frees me to respect who others are and to acknowledge that they have the freedom to pursue their own destinies even as I step to my own drummer. I can be interdependent without being controlled by others and without trying to control them. I am honest with myself and realize that while my ideas may not be right for anyone else they are right for me at this stage of my growth.

Autonomy—Day Seven

I am an original work of art. Unknown

I express my thankfulness for the gift of myself by becoming the person that I was intended to be; by choosing to be me. Today I interject my own style and individuality into this world. I enjoy the *fruits* that I bear: sweet, unique, refreshing apples of gold. I offer them to myself and to others. I am able to recognize the unique contributions that others make to the world community, as well. I respect and appreciate their contributions without feeling in any way diminished by them. We are each uniquely valuable. I am learning to compare myself to me rather than to someone else; to evaluate my growth today in comparison to where I have been. I listen carefully to my internal self-talk tapes about autonomy. When I recognize a negative phrase, I change it. I am accomplishing this exercise more easily and confidently.

Autonomy—Day Eight

There is no better time for joy—than the present time. Lawrence

Today my cup is full of joy. I dip daily into the reservoir, knowing the supply is endless and I can have as much trust, hope and confidence as I can receive. I am experiencing a positive present and am visualizing a successful future. "Non sum qualis eram"—*I am not what I used to be!* I am learning who I am and who I was meant to be and that knowledge frees me to be even more *real.* I no longer need to cover up or pretend. I look for the real reasons behind my actions; see the implications; accept where I have come from; know that I have a choice about where I am going. What freedom that brings! I enjoy being *real.* When I live the truth about who I am, I am empowered.

Identify at least one specific behavior, in relation to autonomy, that you are endeavoring to improve.

Autonomy—Day Nine

List three things you have learned about yourself in relation to autonomy:

- _____

  _____

- _____

  _____

- _____

  _____

Autonomy—Day Ten

Congratulate yourself. You are developing a practical sense of autonomy. Write an affirmation of your unique personal identity:

_____

_____

_____

_____

_____

_____

_____

WILLPOWER

CHAPTER FOUR
UNDERSCORING WILLPOWER

Willpower—Day One

Synonyms: Strength of will, determination, resolution

Antonym: Indecision

The power of *choosing* is the developmental task paired with autonomy. It emerges as we begin to individuate. Learning to activate willpower enables us to make decisions among alternative courses of action and to follow through on our conscious choices. It helps us to develop self-direction and self-governance—abilities that form the basis for resisting temptation. Willed behavior is different from behavior that results from instinct, habit, impulse, or reflex. The latter do not involve conscious choice.

Modern psychologists tend to regard the will as a quality of behavior since it is the whole person who wills. The act of willing involves several components, including:

- The establishment of personal goals, standards, and principles of conduct
- The evaluation of alternative courses of action and the selection of the one that most closely matches our goals, standards, and principles of conduct
- The inhibition of behaviors that conflict with our goals, standards, and principles of conduct
- The perseverance in pursuing our goals and upholding our standards/principles even in the face of obstacles and frustrations.

If we did not learn to develop and appropriately activate willpower, as adults we may find it difficult to make healthy, personal decisions. We may vacillate endlessly between choices and eventually follow the way of least resistance. We may overconform, overcomply, become codependent and exhibit either victim or offender behaviors. If our will was *broken* through misguided pedagogy, we may not possess the skills necessary to create and implement safe, healthy, personal limits. If we possess boundaries at all, they may be either too rigid or too lax.

Ned had a favorite saying, "I can resist anything but temptation." He said this partly in jest and partly in truth. His primary temperament style (as he frequently reminded others) was *not* that of a disciplined, goal-oriented achiever. Unfortunately, Ned had not invested much time or energy in honing the function of willpower. His childhood had been a confusing mixture of indulgence and rigidity. Without clear role-modeling, Ned had not developed the ability to make positive choices and to stick with those choices. He was drifting through life—*rudderless*.

The power of the will resembles muscle power; the more we exercise our wills, the more willpower we have at our disposal and the easier it becomes to use it. With consistent practice, we definitely can develop this ability. Willpower not only assists us in making choices, it helps us to follow through on those choices, as well. The presence or absence of this ability can make a huge difference in our lives.

For example, Sonia dreamed of becoming a professional ice skater. Her parents and her coach explained that while they were willing to teach and encourage her, she herself held the key to success. Did she have the determination to rise at four o'clock in the morning and practice for a couple of hours before leaving for school? Was she willing to learn patterns of self-control in the type of food she ate, the time she went to bed at night, and the restriction of social activities in favor of rehearsal? She not only mobilized the determination but developed the indispensable willpower as well. With that combination, it is not surprising that Sonia eventually shot into the limelight with flashing skates and flying colors.

Arthur made a different choice. His doctors warned him that unless he chose to change his eating patterns, he could expect to develop heart trouble and arteriosclerosis. Arthur loved homemade bread covered with butter and cheese. Such sandwiches were comforting to him, especially when they were followed by a generous bowl of cold, rich ice cream. Because he lacked the willpower to follow through on the recommendations of his physicians, several years later he paid a steep toll—a toll labeled *angioplasty.*

If you need help defining your values, standards, and principles of conduct here is some advice from an unknown author:

Three things to avoid—
Idleness, loquacity, and flippant jesting.
Three things to wish for—
Health, friends, and a cheerful spirit.
Three things to admire—
Intellectual power, dignity, and gratefulness.
Three things to govern—
Temper, tongue, and conduct.
Three things to love—
Courage, gentleness, and affection.
Three things to hate—
Cruelty, arrogance, and ingratitude.
Three things to delight in—
Frankness, freedom, and bravery.

Willpower—Day Two

Table Four—Problems related to willpower   Females—218 Males—102

	Never	Rarely	Sometimes	Frequently	Always
Females	10.5%	30.3%	38.1%	16.5%	4.6%
Males	10.8%	28.4%	30.4%	27.5%	2.9%
Overall	10.6%	29.7%	35.6%	20.0%	4.1%
Me					

Take a few moments to evaluate yourself:

- Do I find it difficult to make personal decisions, usually giving up my purpose and goals to meet the expectations of others?
- Am I able to stick to a personal decision that has been made after thorough thought?
- Are there problems in my life related to willpower?

Willpower—Day Three

Willpower helps us turn our dreams into reality. Taylor

I am making a list of the events in my life that have contributed to my developing a strong, healthy, balanced willpower. Likewise, I am listing the factors that limited my ability to use the power of my will appropriately. I look at these events and factors from a new perspective and I am learning from them. I retain the positive and resolutely let go of the negative. I am the only person *thinking inside my mind.* Today I am using my willpower to help me think nurturing, affirming, and loving thoughts. Whenever negative thoughts surface, I use my willpower to gently direct my thoughts in a positive direction. It is my choice.

Willpower—Day Four

Willpower and a firm determination go hand in hand. Lawrence

According to the laws of aerodynamics, a bumble bee cannot fly. Apparently it does not know about those laws—because it flies. Sometimes I feel like a bumble bee. My background tells me that I am not supposed to fly—and yet, metaphorically, I am determined to do so. My firm determination gives me increased willpower. Today I have a sense of direction and flex my willpower. It is growing stronger and more reliable. My willpower is enabling me to cope effectively with a variety of situations, to make decisions that put negativity behind me. A sense of willpower helps me to avoid feeling *trapped* or *stuck.* Watch out, bumble bee!

Willpower—Day Five

If you stick with this...then you will experience for yourself the truth, and the truth will free you. John 8:31 (TM)

Thoughts of change can trigger fear and resistance. I tap into the strength provided by my Higher Power to help me *let go* of the *not-so-pleasant but familiar* and to risk a change for the better. Today I use my will to make small changes in my life that will lead to bigger changes. I stick with it, choosing to build my willpower day by day. I no longer experience life as simply a series of events over which I have no control. I do have choices. Even choosing not to act is a choice. Life offers me a variety of choices. I am looking for them, evaluating them, and using my willpower to select the ones that are best for me. As my willpower develops in balance, I experience the freedom it gives me. Freedom from exhibiting offender or victim behaviors.

Willpower—Day Six

Great souls have wills;
feeble ones have only wishes. Chinese Proverb

I realize that having an effective, balanced will is vital to success. My willpower is an instrument of success, a bright laser beam that guides me on my chosen path. I no longer spend time rehearsing my mistakes or dwelling upon the shortcomings of others. I no longer anticipate *failure.* Today I am using my willpower to change some of my dreams into reality. I do this by choosing to take one step toward the accomplishment of a goal. I possess willpower and I am managing it rather than allowing it to control me. I feel strong in my self-governance.

Willpower—Day Seven

Success begins with one's will. Unknown

The healthier attitudes that I am developing paint my success in pleasing splashes of vibrant color. Today I check my mental attitudes. I immediately revise any thoughts that would hinder me in my progress. I think of willpower as an electric light switch. The electricity is always available but unless and until I flip the switch on, nothing happens. My state of mind works hand in glove with my willpower. I choose to flip my mental switch on and activate my willpower. With increased practice, I feel stronger, more empowered. I pay attention to the self-talk tapes about willpower that play inside my head. I am recording new, positive self-talk phrases that nurture the development of my willpower.

Willpower—Day Eight

The golden key to success is a balanced willpower. Unknown

I choose to move beyond wishes into action. I am not allowing my willpower to wither away and deteriorate. I use my willpower on a daily basis. I take action—consistently and joyfully. It is empowering to know that I can act (rather than just react) and that I do possess wisdom to act wisely in my behalf. Today I realize that my willpower is becoming a familiar and supportive friend. I realize that "I will" used with wisdom is more important than "IQ." I ask my Higher Power for wisdom on a daily basis. How comforting to know that it is supplied generously and without any harsh feedback! Likewise, I give up finding fault with myself for my past choices. I do not *beat myself up* over poor choices. Rather, I look at the choices I have made and learn from them. Some choices I may choose to repeat; others I will not. My faith in myself grows as I consistently make wiser choices.

Identify at least one specific behavior, in relation to willpower, that you are taking pains to improve.

_____

_____

_____

_____

_____

_____

_____

_____

Willpower—Day Nine

List three truths you have learned about yourself in relation to willpower.

- _____

  _____

- _____

  _____

- _____

  _____

Willpower—Day Ten

Congratulate yourself on the progress you are making to develop an effective willpower. Write down your personal affirmation regarding willpower.

_____

_____

_____

_____

_____

_____

SELF-ESTEEM

CHAPTER FIVE
AUGMENTING SELF-ESTEEM

Self-Esteem—Day One

Synonyms: Self-worth, self-respect, dignity, self-regard

Antonyms: Self-hatred, self-disrespect, loathing

The power of personal *value* is believed to be in place by the age of three. We established this initial estimate of our individual worth based on the way in which we were treated by others and on what we heard said about us. A positive, balanced sense of self-worth enables us to confidently play a successful role on the stage of life, to respect and love ourselves, and to thrive.

We likely developed an optimum level of self-esteem if we:

- had role-models who possessed positive levels of self-esteem
- were respected as individuals
- were encouraged to like ourselves
- heard people say positive, nurturing things to us and about us
- believed that we were valued simply because we existed (apart from our performance or conformance).

On the other hand, if we came from a dysfunctional background we may have failed to develop a healthy sense of self. We may have learned to be *us*—but not *me*. If there was constant tension, major trauma, stress, and frequent crises within our family-of-origin, we may have perceived that we were somehow inadequate. In such an environment we likely developed self-esteem problems and learned to exhibit behaviors that fall around a circular continuum: sometimes feeling abysmally worthless and sometimes behaving as if we are much better than others.

If we failed to develop a healthy level of self-worth, as adults we are at risk for looking outside ourselves to find validation—to feel okay about ourselves. We are at risk for becoming inappropriately dependent upon whatever person, place, thing, substance, activity, or process makes us feel better about ourselves—a search that can lead to addictive behaviors.

Jeannette was in the habit of trying to make herself feel better about herself by recounting the mistakes of others. Joel, her boyfriend, was in the same boat. At their engagement party, a friend presented them with a plaque that read: "If I am OK with me, I have no need to find fault with you." It was a timely gesture to remind them both that without developing healthy levels of self-worth and breaking the habit of criticizing others in order to bolster their own sense of value, their relationship wouldn't develop into a healthy, productive, rewarding partnership.

Lillian's self-esteem was so low that she agonized for days over what casserole to prepare for the Thanksgiving potluck at school. Finally she decided on her family's favorite dish but then tried to obtain verbal assurance from several individuals ahead of time that they would like the casserole. This incident became a learning experience for her when a friend took the time to point out that spurned dishes are not necessarily a statement about the cook. People usually pamper their taste buds. If we feel good about ourselves we can contribute to a potluck without taking personal offense if someone prefers another casserole.

The good news is that while we were not responsible for our initial sense of self-worth, we are completely responsible for our continuing level of self-esteem. If we have problems in this area, it can be helpful to understand our inestimable worth to God. This can help us to value ourselves appropriately and to be willing to invest the time and energy needed to develop a healthy sense of self-esteem. As we reparent ourselves, we can role-model our balanced self-worth. We can encourage others to appreciate their value, as well. We can use our influence to prevent the development of self-esteem problems in children.

In order to develop an optimal level of self-esteem we need to identify the messages we received about ourselves from early childhood onward. We need to compare those messages with what we are learning about ourselves individually, in the present. We need to make decisions about:

- Whether or not our present level of self-esteem is optimum
- The messages about ourselves that we will keep versus those to be discarded
- The new beliefs about ourselves that may need to be developed
- The type of people with whom we choose to associate on a daily basis
- The personal boundaries we will set.

Our life is a collection of events and thoughts. What we think about the events is usually of greater importance than the events themselves. We are what we think about all day long—fifty-thousand thoughts at a minimum. We can harness those thoughts to work for us in building and maintaining optimum self-esteem.

Self-Esteem—Day Two

Table Five—Problems related to self-esteem   Females—218 Males—102

	Never	Rarely	Sometimes	Frequently	Always
Females	6.9%	18.8%	39.9%	28.0%	6.4%
Males	17.6%	26.5%	21.5%	27.5%	6.9%
Overall	10.3%	21.2%	34.1%	27.8%	6.6%
Me					

Take a few moments to evaluate yourself:

- Do I constantly feel that others are better than I am in appearance, in poise, in confidence, in competence, et cetera?
- Do I believe that I am better than others?
- Do I make direct eye-contact with others and speak confidently to them?
- Does my posture portray the belief that I am valuable and worthwhile or does it reflect poor self-esteem?
- Are there problems in my life related to self-esteem issues?

Self-Esteem—Day Three

*Each day of my life is a precious gem
set with golden opportunities. Lawrence*

I am making a list of the events in my life that have contributed to my developing an optimum level of self-worth. Likewise, I am listing the factors that influenced me to develop self-esteem problems. I am looking at these events and factors from a new perspective. The information I am gleaning is of inestimable value to me. I can keep the positive and gently let go of the negative. Today I choose to develop a positive, balanced sense of self-worth. I know it is possible to do so. It is my choice. Every golden moment of my life is replete with jewels of opportunities. I am worthy of those jewels. I recognize their value. I accept the opportunities they present.

Self-Esteem—Day Four

*No one can make us feel a particular
way without our assent. Anonymous*

Just because others choose to believe certain things about me does not mean that those beliefs are accurate. They are simply opinions —of other human beings who are not infallible. It is within my power to hold onto those opinions or to let them go. Today I know that no one can make me feel valueless without my consent. I choose to feel neither inferior nor superior to others. I choose to be me. Those who need to know the truth about me will see who I am. I need not try to *prove* anything to myself or to others. I simply need to be me and keep adding building blocks to the superstructure of my self-worth. I do not build carelessly or in vain. During this process I pay attention to my internal self-talk tapes about self-esteem. I am rehearsing thoughts and words that help me to build a healthy sense of self-esteem. These messages are replayed continually whether or not I am consciously aware of them. They help me to treat myself with worth and dignity.

Self-Esteem—Day Five

Make no mistake, our opinion in life, of
what we can be, surely shapes us. Unknown

I am responsible for the way in which I view myself. I cannot wait for others to affirm or deny my worth. Today I give myself the perpetual gift of unconditional acceptance. I see myself as a new baby to be loved, nurtured, and protected at all costs. I choose to believe (and to *feel*) that I am precious and honored. I am worthy to take this journey of life simply because I exist. I know that nothing is ever accomplished until someone is convinced that it needs to be done and believes that now is the time to do it. I am convinced that I need to build an optimum sense of self-esteem. I believe that now is the time to do it. Therefore, I begin. I begin with who I am and move forward from there. My belief in my intrinsic value is already enhancing the state of my self-esteem.

Self-Esteem—Day Six

Don't ask, "Who does someone else think
I am?" Rather, ask yourself, "Who am I?" Taylor

I am living in reality, looking honestly for the truth about myself and about my private world. I rest assured that moment by moment I am doing the best I can right now. I recognize the progress I have made since yesterday; I chart my goal for tomorrow. For today, I am asking myself the often avoided question, "Who am I?" I truly want to know. I cannot validate myself until I know myself. My goal is to be able to totally approve of myself and my behaviors. It's nice when others approve of me but their approval is not necessary to my well being; neither is it necessary for me to seek the approval of everyone. This is a journey of discovery. There is no turning back. I do not fear it; I strive to understand it.

Self-Esteem—Day Seven

*Each of you must take responsibility for doing the
creative best you can with your own life. Galatians 6:4*

My truest wealth on earth consists of who I am. I am a treasure and
do not treat myself with indifference or with contempt. I am
learning the difference between acknowledging my weaknesses
and *putting myself down* for them. I accept my strengths with
pleasure and my weaknesses with grace. Today I cut the gangrene
of personal contempt out of my life. I am magnanimous enough to
forgive myself for making mistakes. I store up treasure by
becoming the person I was designed to be. I accept all that entails,
knowing there is no one else in this world exactly like me. I realize
that unless I honor my self-worth, it will not honored by others.

Self-Esteem—Day Eight

Fake it til you make it. Old Adage

My efforts to develop a healthy level of self-worth stand me in
good stead when others criticize me. I view their suggestions as
flower petals that have been dropped into my hand. Gently I sift
through them, keeping the ones by which I can benefit—and gently
blowing the rest away. Today I know who I am and I feel good
about who I am. In my mind's eye, I see the person I am becoming
and I am acting that picture out now. When others disapprove of
my behavior or a choice that I have made, I lean on my internal
confidence. I know that I chose the best way I could think of at the
time. Another day I may make a different choice. I always have
that option. It is enough.

Identify at least one behavior, in relation to self-esteem, that you
are striving to improve.

_____

_____

Self-esteem—Day Nine

List three details you have learned about yourself in relation to self-esteem.

- _____

_____

- _____

_____

- _____

_____

Self-Esteem—Day Ten

Aren't you proud of the way in which you are working to develop an optimum level of self-esteem? Keep up the good work! Write down your personal affirmation of self-esteem.

_____

_____

_____

_____

_____

_____

OTHER-ESTEEM

CHAPTER SIX
ADVANCING OTHER-ESTEEM

Other-Esteem—Day One

Synonyms: Respect for humanity, regard for others, consideration

Antonyms: Human disregard, indifference to others

The power of valuing others is the task paired with self-esteem. In reality, we treat others as we treat ourselves; we value and respect others to the degree that we value and respect ourselves.

Learning to respect and esteem others enables us to genuinely affirm them for who they are and for what they accomplish in life without our feeling threatened; without our perceiving that in some way their success diminishes us.

If we fail to esteem others, we are at risk for becoming overcompetitive, jealous, envious, and even immobile. We may avoid developing the skills for effective teamwork and cooperation. We will likely exhibit critical, judgmental behaviors and generally have a tendency to *tear down* rather than to *build up*.

Two people stepped off the curb as the light changed to green. A car running a red light nearly struck them. "You idiot! You could have killed us," screamed the first person, shaking a fist angrily at the careening car.

The second responded by saying, "We are indeed fortunate that model of car handles so well!" The contrasting responses reflected perspectives based on each pedestrian's personal level of self-esteem.

We can help to build self-esteem in others by devoting a portion of our time to supporting and applauding them, genuinely rejoicing in their success rather than selfishly trying to star only ourselves. The principal of an inner-city middle school uses this principle on a regular basis. Within the short space of a couple of years, she has improved the school's success rate in a number of areas: the number of drop-outs has diminished, college acceptance rates have improved, student employment has increased, the number of student arrests and jail sentences has decreased, unwed pregnancies are at an all time low, and there is now a waiting list of entrants to the school.

How has she done this? The key has been to applaud rather than criticize the students. Often we concentrate on the mistakes of others rather than on applauding their successes. Faculty members consistently look for ways to praise even small successes. According to the principal, this strategy has made all the difference.

Nations spend a small fortune developing, implementing, enforcing, and litigating laws concerning property, payment of debts, and compensation for injury/damage because individuals do not respect others or their property. Most, if not all, the wrongs against other individuals including battery, theft, adultery, and murder could be prevented if everyone truly esteemed others.

We can look for ways to validate the efforts and successes of others even as we are learning how to validate our own personal growth. Even when outcomes are not what we desired, we can reward effort. Human beings often invest a great deal of effort in projects that do not pan out as expected and generally, most people have a tendency to reward only desired outcomes.

Separating effort from outcome enables us to see opportunities for offering nurturing and validation in almost every situation. We can learn new affirmative phrases, practice them ahead of time, and then say them aloud to others as appropriate— accelerating their process of developing these new behaviors as well.

Henry Ward Beecher understood the importance of valuing and affirming others. He wrote:

> Do not keep the alabaster boxes of
> your love and tenderness sealed up
> until your friends are dead. Fill their
> lives with sweetness. Speak
> approving, cheering words while
> their ears can hear them and while
> their hearts can be thrilled by them.

Other-Esteem—Day Two

Table Six—Problems related to other-esteem   Females—216 Males—102

	Never	Rarely	Sometimes	Frequently	Always
Females	10.2%	39.4%	34.7%	13.9%	1.8%
Males	13.7%	32.4%	39.2%	12.7%	2.0%
Overall	11.3%	37.1%	36.2%	13.5%	1.9%
Me					

Take a few moments to evaluate yourself:

- Do I consistently treat others with respect and dignity?
- Does their age, gender, status or position influence my attitude toward them?
- Do I try to make myself feel better by finding fault with others or putting them down?
- Are there problems in my life related to other-esteem?

Other-Esteem—Day Three

Love your neighbor as yourself. Luke 10:27

I am making a list of the events in my life that have contributed to my learning to consider and value others. Likewise, I am listing the factors that influenced me to develop a lack of consideration and esteem for others. I look at these events and factors from a new perspective and I am learning from them. I can cherish the positive and chuck the negative. Today I know that I am truly loved and valued by my Higher Power and I choose to pass along this acceptance to others. I am finding opportunities to affirm others; to help them feel good about themselves. The more I do this, the less desperately I crave approval from others. Because I am learning how to validate them, I find it even easier to validate myself and encourage myself in this journey.

Other-Esteem—Day Four

*How we treat others gives us neither rewards
nor punishments—only consequences. Unknown*

I willingly open my heart and let understanding flood into my mind. I realize that the way in which I esteem others is but a reflection of the value I place upon myself. The collage of previous experiences and learned attitudes unfolds before me. Me, myself, and I are learning together. I do not waste time on regrets and wishing *if only.* I face the events that have happened to me in the past and use them as stepping-stones. I am able to do this. I choose to do this. I am making choices to develop confidence in myself and my Higher Power. I am opening my life to the beauty of esteeming others. This does not mean that I will like or accept the behaviors of another, or that I will choose to subject myself to those behaviors. I choose to place great value on others simply because they exist, even as I place great value on myself simply because I exist.

Other-Esteem—Day Five

*One kind word driven home is far better
than three left to languish on base. Anonymous*

Today I purpose to exhibit traits of nonabrasiveness in my contact with others. I choose to show them by my actions that they are valuable and important. I am learning how to apply myself on this journey. I am listening for words of wisdom. Everyone has something to teach. Every lesson contains a seed pearl. I am learning to watch for them. Nothing is wasted. It is amazing; everywhere I turn I find help. I know that I am no better than anyone else; I am no worse, although we may each have different abilities and make different contributions. I am valuable simply because I am. That knowledge frees me to become all that I can become; to share my uniqueness when and where it is appropriate and when and where it will be valued. The more I apply myself, the easier it becomes. The more I listen for knowledge, the more I hear.

Other-Esteem—Day Six

Whenever you try to hold someone else back,
you end up being held back, as well. Unknown

Today I am learning that life can be a win-win experience. I do not try to hold others back. Instead, we walk forward together. I am not diminished by the successes of others; together we are all enriched. Figuratively speaking, I dig deep within myself and honor the sprouting seed that I discover there. Although it is but a seedling, I can see the tree that it is becoming; a strong, unique, fruitful, and mature tree. The seedling and I are one. The tree and I are also one. We are in process. Because I do this for myself I can honor the process in others. I cannot always control what happens to me; I can control my response to what happens to me. In the same way, I rejoice with those who rejoice. That in and of itself is a win-win position.

Other-Esteem—Day Seven

We tend to treat ourselves the way we were treated—
and to treat others the way we treat ourselves. Taylor

I am carefully listening to my internal self-talk tapes about other-esteem, paying attention to what I hear and evaluating each phrase for its potential to nurture and affirm or to discourage and sabotage. When I recognize a negative phrase that would prompt me to devalue others, I make a decision to change it. I turn-down the volume on old unhelpful messages, especially those that tempt me to expend energy finding fault with others. Today I concentrate on recording new, positive self-talk messages. I am rehearsing thoughts and words that help me to honor the intrinsic worth of others—just as they are. These messages are replayed continually whether or not I am consciously aware of them. Thus they influence my thoughts and my behaviors. I am treating others with respect because I respect myself. I offer them affirmation because I know how to affirm myself.

Other-Esteem—Day Eight

If you help, just help, don't take over...if you give
encouraging guidance...don't get bossy. Romans 12:6-8 (TM)

I now know that it is possible to change the way I view myself; to fully recognize my individual self-worth. Understanding my value does not diminish that of another nor does it set up a situation of comparison. Understanding my worth and potential simply enables me to better appreciate the worth and potential of others. Today I continue on my journey of creating the possible (optimum self-esteem) from the seemingly impossible (the self-esteem problems with which I began). After all, a diamond is simply a piece of coal that, when under pressure, endured. I already see many diamonds in my life, each with many fine facets.

Identify one specific behavior, related to esteeming others, that you have targeted for improvement.

_____

_____

_____

_____

Other-esteem can also involve honoring other forms of life. Bob Folkenberg tells a wonderful story about a young boy and his father who were at the beach. The night before, a windstorm had raged along the coast. Hundreds of starfish had been washed ashore. The little fellow was running around picking up starfish and throwing them back into the ocean.

As he threw another starfish into the water his father said, "Son, why waste your time throwing that starfish into the ocean? It won't make any difference. Look, there are hundreds of them on the beach!"

His son paused a second and then replied, "Well, it made all the difference in the world to that starfish."

Other-Esteem—Day Nine

List three things you have learned about yourself in relation to other-esteem.

● _____

_____

● _____

_____

● _____

_____

Other-Esteem—Day Ten

Learning to esteem others as individuals—simply because they exist and separate from the behaviors they exhibit—is a learned skill. Write down your personal affirmation of other-esteem.

_____

_____

_____

_____

_____

_____

PURPOSE

CHAPTER SEVEN
NURTURING PURPOSE

Purpose—Day One

Synonyms: Aim, aspiration, ambition

Antonym: Irresolution

The power of *goal-setting* is a developmental task that takes root during the fourth and fifth years of life. Learning to be purposeful enables us to set goals for ourselves and to recognize those of others. It helps us to see the *big picture* and to manage present realities in the light of future possibilities.

Kevin McCarthy, author of *THE ON-PURPOSE PERSON*, says, "Nothing adds more fullness and meaning to life than discovering your purpose and living it out seven days a week!" If we did not learn purpose, as adults we may have difficulty setting goals in life; may even be unable to recognize the long-term value of goal-setting. We may drift along without any particular aim. We may be unable to control gratification of our wants in the present.

We have found it helpful to study the lives of Bible personalities, to discover how they exhibited purpose or the lack thereof. The life of Queen Esther is a favorite. Her ability to follow through on her goal resulted in the rescue of an entire nation from destruction. The life stories of Joseph and Moses are also favorites. Their ability to follow through on their goals enabled Joseph to feed the country's entire population during seven years of famine and helped Moses to transport an entire nation from Egypt to Canaan.

We have also found it helpful to look around us in our present world and identify individuals who have exhibited purpose. We can study their techniques and watch them set and achieve goals. Take Alex Haley for example, the author of *ROOTS*. He had heard the haunting stories of slavery passed down through many generations in America. This prompted him to discover the beginning of his family line and he spent years in painstaking research—piecing the stories together. His work included a trip to

Africa and from this man's pilgrimage came not only a book but a gripping television series. One man's purpose benefited a multitude.

Likewise, we can notice those around us whose lives appear to have no purpose and we can learn from their experiences as well. Above all, we can strive to achieve a balance. We can choose not to drift along in life without a defined purpose in mind. Neither will we pursue success in a way that steps on others or that leaves no time for us to smell the roses along the way.

One way in which to begin developing purpose is to take stock of our lives; where we have come from and where we want to go. We can write down one personal long-term goal and then divide that goal into smaller short-term goals. Every day we can take one step toward accomplishing a short-term goal. It is absolutely amazing how, little by little, those smaller steps eventually translate into the accomplishment of a bigger step and the realization of an even larger long-term goal.

We are often accustomed to helping small children break a task down into small steps. For example, initially we give them the toothbrush with the toothpaste already applied. Later we teach them the process as a sequence of small steps: pick up the toothpaste tube, take off the cap, squeeze a small amount onto the brush, turn on the water, et cetera.

We sometimes forget this model when dealing with ourselves and with other adults. Just because we are grown physically does not mean that we automatically know the best way to achieve completion of every task. We can ask for help in identifying the steps necessary to accomplish a task; we can provide as well as accept assistance.

Sometimes we limit ourselves by thinking of goals only in relation to a career, vacation plans, or some object we desire to possess. Goal setting is best integrated into every aspect of our lives. Take a few minutes and define several areas in which you want to set goals. Some may be long-term goals, others short-term, still others may involve a philosophy by which to live. An unknown writer outlined some worthy goals as follows:

Silence - when your words could hurt.
Patience - when your neighbor's curt.

Deafness - when the scandal flows.
Thoughtfulness - for others' woes.
Promptness - when stern duty calls.
Courage - when misfortune falls.

Purpose—Day Two

Table Seven—Problems related to purpose   Females—216 Males—102

	Never	Rarely	Sometimes	Frequently	Always
Females	19.9%	37.5%	24.1%	15.8%	2.7%
Males	16.7%	34.3%	31.4%	9.8%	7.8%
Overall	18.9%	36.5%	26.4%	13.8%	4.4%
Me					

Take a few moments to evaluate yourself:

- Have I daily challenged myself by setting some specific goals to accomplish?
- Do I greet each day with apathy, my only goal being to make it through the next twenty-four hours?
- Have I developed some goals in every area of my life: personal, relational, career, spiritual, educational?
- Are there problems in my life related to purpose or goal-setting?

Purpose—Day Three

What I have planned, that will I do. Isaiah 46:11

I am making a list of the events in my life that have contributed to my developing an ability to set goals in my life, to develop a sense of purpose. Likewise, I am listing the factors that influenced me to develop problems in the area of goal-setting. I look at these events and factors from a new perspective and I am learning from them. I can nurture the positive and gently remove the negative. Today I have set myself one achievable goal and I am breaking that goal down into small, manageable steps. I am taking one of those small steps right now by repeating this affirmation aloud. I take another small step as I act upon this affirmation.

Purpose—Day Four

We can do no great things—
only small things with great love. Mother Teresa

Lasting change usually occurs through a series of small successes. Today I am looking inside myself and checking my attitude, the attitude with which I approach my tasks. I am truly honest and I am making the necessary adjustments so that I work positively. I approach each small step or task with love. This mind-set helps me to manage stress more effectively and to avoid unnecessary expenditure of energy. This positive attitude helps me to be content with my growth today. Today's growth is a *small thing* but it is what I can do. And because I do it positively and lovingly, my journey continues toward the goals about which I dream so vividly.

Purpose—Day Five

Whatever your hand finds to do,
do it with your might. Ecclesiastes 9:10

Energy flows through me into my tasks. I can concentrate clearly on projects, enjoying the process of doing and seeing them through to conclusion. I am alert to what needs to be accomplished in my life. I am learning to set goals; thinking before acting. I am resisting the temptation to try to set and accomplish goals at one fell swoop. Rather, I am engaging in the process a little at a time. Because I have worked on developing trust, hope, autonomy, and willpower; because I respect myself and others, I am easily accomplishing what I have planned. I enjoy the tasks that make up today and I am completing them enthusiastically. By applying all my might to each worthy endeavor, I find myself less distracted than previously. I am developing the habit of initiative and it is steadfastly snowballing.

Purpose—Day Six

*Aim high. You may not attain all your goals but
you will accomplish more than if you aim low. Unknown*

Because of my past conditioning, I have not always *aimed high.*
The goals I did have were not always high caliber. I am filtering
out the negative ideas that impede my progress. Today I am
making a list of three goals for myself. All are of high caliber but
one of these really aims high. I am writing down the steps that I'll
need to take in order to achieve those goals. Each day I use my
willpower to do at least one thing that can help me to take one of
those steps (e.g., make a phone call, write a letter, read a chapter of
a book, contact someone who can assist me, enroll in a course). I
choose to aim high! I choose to take wing—high above the
cacophony of dysfunction that pervades so much of society. I can
do it. I am not immobilized by obstacles because I keep my eyes
fixed on my goals.

Purpose—Day Seven

I press on toward the goal. Philippians 3:14

I believe that one of God's purposes for me is that I become the
person I am able to become. I am learning how to take small steps
well—because they will determine my outcome. Today I carefully
select my thoughts and harbor only those that will help me to
accomplish my desired goals. I walk through my day successfully,
setting my schedule with confidence that I am going to accomplish
the necessary daily tasks. I am proving my abilities to myself and
as this happens, others notice my self-confidence as well. They see
my daily achievements and show confidence in me. I am carefully
listening to my internal self-talk related to purpose. When I
recognize a negative phrase, I immediately make a decision to
develop positive self-talk messages. They help me to stay centered
about my goal-setting. I move forward toward the promised prize.

Purpose—Day Eight

Give to the world the best you have
and the best will come back to you. Proverb

Beliefs are powerful. Like blueprints from my past, they influence my life today. When I only partially believe that life is worth living, my efforts are half-hearted, unbalanced, and distorted. Today I believe with all my heart that my life is well worth living. I *see* what a full and meaningful life I can experience. With this belief clearly in mind, all that I do leads me in that direction. What I believe, I become. I focus clearly on the goals I have established. I see the person I am becoming rising from the indecisiveness of my past. I firmly believe that I deserve to be happy. I am creating that sense of happiness right now.

Identify one specific behavior, in relation to purpose, on which you are currently working.

_____

_____

_____

_____

_____

_____

Purpose—Day Nine

List three realities you have learned about yourself in regard to purpose.

- _____

  _____

- _____

  _____

- _____

  _____

Purpose—Day Ten

You are _hanging in there_ on your personal growth journey. It takes some discipline, doesn't it? Remember, the rewards are built in. Write down your personal affirmation related to purpose.

_____

_____

_____

_____

_____

_____

_____

INITIATIVE

CHAPTER EIGHT
FOSTERING INITIATIVE

Initiative—Day One

Synonyms: Drive, energy, ambition

Antonym: Laziness

The power of taking constructive *action* is the developmental task paired with purpose. Learning initiative enables us to take steps to accomplish a goal. It involves developing a sense that we are capable of productively participating in life and of following through on our decisions.

If we were overcontrolled during childhood and our attempts at initiative were squelched, we may not have developed a sense of ability to take action in life. If we did not learn initiative, as adults we may not be able to take care of the self properly. We may perceive that we are incompetent or inadequate.

Argenta was congratulating a childhood friend on earning a doctorate. "I barely finished high school, myself," she laughed. "What do you suppose makes the difference between the two of us? I'm sure that I'm just as smart as you are!"

Her friend replied thoughtfully, "I don't think brains have anything to do with it. The main difference may be that I took the initiative to enroll in night school—while you only talked about doing it some day." Desire isn't enough; wishing won't accomplish goals. We have to take action. Researchers say that when we consistently implement and practice a new behavior for twenty-one days in a row, we'll be well on our way to developing a new habit. Just imagine, by consistently choosing to take action on a daily basis, you can be well on your way to developing initiative before you know it!

Individual drops of water join together to form a little rivulet, that gradually joins others to form a stream, that eventually joins still others to create a rushing river, that eventually makes its way to the mighty sea. Just so with us. Many tiny actions purposefully initiated enable us to take a small step; that enables us to take a larger step; that allows us to climb to another level of maturity; that permits us to accomplish major goals. But we have to take *action*. As the old saying goes, wishing without working is like canoeing without paddling; you drift along and don't really go anywhere.

It is amazing to realize that one year from now we can look back and see that we have accomplished a great deal—just by taking constructive action—while many others will still be talking about what they wish they could do and wondering how others managed to accomplish what they did.

In a similar way, collective initiative can often accomplish what would be impossible individually. For example, a poor congregation in Africa needed a new church building. They selected a site several hundred feet above the riverbed that would provide them with clay and rock. Each family was assigned the responsibility to transport several loads of rock and clay to the building site. Through collective initiative, the building project was completed in less than a year.

We can begin improving our initiative by compiling a short list of tasks that need to be accomplished. Then we can select one of them and implement willpower to take action toward its completion. Remember that initiative is a choice. For some, that may mean choosing to break the habit of laziness or procrastination. For others, it may mean stretching just a little bit farther than usual. It was Robert Browning who challenged us to believe that our reach should exceed our grasp. We'll never know our full potential until we venture out.

Initiative—Day Two

Table Eight—Problems related to initiative   Females—217 Males—102

	Never	Rarely	Sometimes	Frequently	Always
Females	19.8%	36.4%	29.5%	11.1%	3.2%
Males	15.7%	32.3%	31.4%	16.7%	3.9%
Overall	18.5%	35.1%	30.1%	12.8%	3.4%
Me					

Take a few moments to evaluate yourself:

- Do I confidently take action to attack projects and bring them to completion?
- Do I frequently procrastinate, avoiding taking action even when I know that it would be beneficial to me?
- Are there problems in my life related to initiative?

Initiative—Day Three

Surely you will reward each person according to what he/she has done. Psalm 62:11

I am making a list of the events in my life that have contributed to my developing an ability to take action in life. Likewise, I am listing the factors that influenced me to develop problems in the area of initiative. I look at these events and factors from a new perspective and I am learning from them. I choose to nurture the positive and abandon the negative. There is something in my life that I need to make *better*—and I am beginning *now.* Delay and procrastination now make me uncomfortable. Today I am learning to commence action! I am taking positive, healthy, necessary steps to better my life. I take the initiative to plan my journey, to take action, and to see that my goals are realized.

Initiative—Day Four

The way to get ahead is to get started—now. Unknown

I am learning that it is more effective to take one small step today than to just think about what I wish my status would be like twelve months from now. It is important to move from theory into practice; to actually try out one idea rather than to collect a thousand ideas and never implement any of them. Today I am devoting thirty minutes to this project; thirty minutes that will help me to progress. I allow no interruptions; I focus my whole attention. It is exciting to realize that what I am doing today will pay rich dividends in the future. Knowledge has power only when it is actually used. I use what I know.

Initiative—Day Five

Success is more likely to be the result of
initiative and hard work than of talent. Old Saying

I am truly internalizing the truth that in order for me to accomplish a large goal, I must begin by accomplishing small goals. A toddler's first steps usually follow many failed attempts. And there were many days of crawling preceding those! It is somewhat like the old riddle, "How does one eat an elephant? One bite at a time." Today I am taking another small step toward reaching a long-term goal. When I feel tired or momentarily discouraged, I remember that my Higher Power supports me. I am not taking this journey alone. I am not taking action alone. This is a comforting thought. I welcome the changes that are occurring and no longer waste my energies pursuing a life that was unpleasant but tolerable because I was so accustomed to it. As I become aware of inner promptings, I act immediately to set priorities that help me to take constructive action.

Initiative—Day Six

Each problem has hidden within it an
opportunity so powerful that it literally dwarfs
the problem. Our task is to look beyond the problem—
to discover and embrace the opportunity. Ancient Proverb

I realize that the present moment is of utmost importance. What I do now will contribute to or detract from my future outcome. I cannot change what happened yesterday; I cannot guarantee what will happen tomorrow; I only have today in which to act. Therefore, I devote my attention to present activities, prioritizing the small steps and seeing them through to completion. I do not know what tomorrow might bring. I can see the *now* and feel the satisfaction that comes from paying attention to the present. I am not afraid to succeed. Victory is assured; it is no longer necessary to snatch it from the jaws of defeat. My success is planned. Already I am experiencing the results of steps that I am taking in my journey toward developing initiative.

Initiative—Day Seven

A longing fulfilled is sweet to the soul. Proverbs 13:19

I am learning to define the difference between my *needs* and my wants. I am taking responsibility for meeting those needs as well as some of my wants. Today I am giving myself the opportunity and the permission to fulfill one wish before it is time for me to go to sleep. This is a gift I am giving myself; a gift of encouragement and nurturing; a gift that recognizes that I am worthy of having some of my longings fulfilled—a sweet bonus. I purpose to give myself a bonus gift every day and, whenever possible, give one to someone else. This gift may be as simple as a smile, a hand-written note, or a pat of encouragement. I am carefully listening to my internal self-talk tapes about initiative. I pay attention to what I hear and evaluate each phrase for its potential to improve or diminish my initiative. When I recognize a negative phrase that would sabotage my personal growth, I make a decision to change it. I *turn down* the volume on old, unhelpful messages and concentrate instead on recording new, positive self-talk messages.

Initiative—Day Eight

*Don't be afraid to go out on
a limb; that's where the fruit is. Axiom*

I am looking at my *mistakes* in a new way. They are simply labels and judgments that we, as human beings, assign to situations and actions that have already taken place. A failure, a mistake is not a tragedy. It is an event that may have saved me (as well as others who were observing) from taking a thousand steps in the wrong direction. When something in my life seems not to have turned out as I envisioned or desired, I am now able to look at it more objectively. Today I select one of those *mistakes* and evaluate what went awry. Metaphorically, I stretch toward the end of the limb. I look for another way in which to approach the same or a similar situation in order to achieve a more appropriate outcome. I am fearless in this endeavor.

Identify one specific behavior, in relation to initiative, you are trying to improve.

_____

_____

_____

_____

_____

Initiative—Day Nine

Today, list three lessons you have learned about yourself in relation to initiative.

- _____

_____

- _____

_____

- _____

_____

Initiative—Day Ten

Recognize the positive changes in your life that are accruing because you are learning to take constructive *action*. Write down your personal affirmation related to initiative.

_____

_____

_____

_____

_____

_____

_____

_____

_____

_____

_____

_____

AESTHESIA

CHAPTER NINE
GUIDING AESTHESIA

Aesthesia—Day One

Synonyms: Sensitivity, sensations

Antonym: Apathy

The power of managing our *emotions and feelings* is a developmental task that influences all facets of life. Learning to identify, experience, and appropriately manage the entire range of emotions and feelings available to human beings, enables us to experience life in all of its colorful fullness. This ability allows us to take corrective action as necessary based on the cues our body gives us.

If we did not learn how to effectively manage all our emotions and feelings, as adults we are at risk for overreacting or underreacting instead of responding appropriately. The energy generated by emotions, if not dissipated or handled correctly, can adversely affect us physically, intellectually, emotionally, sexually, and spiritually. It can discolor our internal world as well as spill out and negatively impact our external world.

It can be helpful to describe emotions and feelings as somewhat separate entities. Emotions are physiological changes in the body that result from a stimulus to the brain's limbic system. Those physiological changes are interpreted into feelings in the cerebrum. We *think* about those changes, assign relative importance to them, and label them. For example, we identify the emotion of joy and describe ourselves as feeling delighted, blessed, satisfied, or happy. In general, we translate our emotions into feelings based on our past experience, knowledge base, habit patterns, and lessons learned in our family of origin. While we may not always be responsible for the surfacing of initial emotions, we are responsible for our feelings and for the behaviors we choose to exhibit based on those feelings.

In group therapy, Carl was amazed to learn that he could choose to experience all his emotions and feelings without acting upon any of them. He was most familiar with the emotion of anger and alternated between suppressing it and letting it all hang out. Another group member, Nell, discovered that she had carried the sadness for her entire family; Steve had carried the fear in his family.

The only acceptable emotion in Ruth's family had been joy. She had been taught that a good Christian is always happy. Since her father was the senior pastor in a large Christian church, Ruth learned to appear happy and to stifle not only appropriate feelings of grief but all tears, as well. Actually, she had spent forty-five years crying on the inside—and feeling *guilty* about it. One of the group members reminded her that the shortest sentence in the Bible consists of only two words: Jesus wept (John 11:35). Ruth had never realized this!

The group members learned that emotions are simply *flags* to get our attention. For example, the emotion of anger signals that our boundaries have been invaded; the emotion of fear, that a threat to our personal safety may be present. The emotion of sadness alerts us to a loss in our lives that needs to be grieved and healed. The emotion of joy indicates that we are successfully managing the routine glitches and stresses on the screen of life in a manner that allows us to sense a deep, calm, contentment.

Euphoria is a flag that pops up occasionally when something especially stimulating or unusually exciting happens. Some individuals mistakenly believe that they can live in a state of unceasing ecstasy. They even try to artificially achieve a perpetual high through the use of mind-altering substances. The human organism was not designed to experience euphoria on a continual basis. This would result in exhaustion. Euphoria is meant to be the spice of life, not life itself.

How we interpret our emotions into feelings and what we do with them is exceedingly important. Outside of injury or illness involving brain structure and chemistry, managing emotions and feelings successfully is an acquired skill. In general:

- We learn how to (or how not to) identify and experience all emotions and feelings. This means we choose, for example, how badly we will feel and for how long we will remain at that level

- We choose whether or not we will act upon our feelings as well as the type and intensity of relative behaviors we will exhibit
- We can learn a new, more functional way of dealing with our emotions and feelings if we want to do so
- In order to change the way we *feel,* we need to change the way we *think.*

It is important to avoid hanging onto and continually waving the flags of anger, fear, and sadness. When we drive down the highway and see an orange flag ahead, we need to pay attention and be ready to take appropriate action. Perhaps there is a large hole in the pavement, a mud slide, or a vehicle accident ahead. As we drive by the flag, we do not reach out, grab the flag, and wave it wildly as we continue down the highway. We notice it, take appropriate action, leave it behind, and gratefully continue on our journey.

A first step in learning to manage our emotions and feelings appropriately is to identify our beliefs about them. Who taught them to us? Were they valid during childhood? Are they still valid during adulthood? Unless we do family-of-origin work in this area, we are at risk for simply perpetuating the beliefs and attitudes that we absorbed as children—usually prior to the age of five. Some of them may be desirable, others may not. Erroneous beliefs can prevent us from learning to manage our emotions and feelings successfully. In fact, they can be formidable adversaries. As Sally Kempton pointed out, "It's hard to fight an enemy who has an outpost in your head."

A second step is to evaluate our usual facial expression on a daily basis. "Are you sad today?" a little child asked her mother.

No," my dear, "I'm quite happy today," she replied.

"Well, then," the child continued, "you need to tell your face about it."

Author Justice Blair writes in his book *WHO GETS SICK,* that "if we assume a facial expression of happiness we can increase blood flow to the brain and stimulate release of favorable neurotransmitters." When our faces shape a smile—even more so when we are smiling internally as well—our immune system is boosted. The level of the antibody, Immune Gobulin A (IgA), designed to provide localized protection on mucous membranes, increases.

Researchers tell us that it takes thirteen facial muscles to create a smile; thirty-seven to frown. Why would anyone take the extra energy to perpetually frown? Perhaps one of the reasons that most people are attracted to babies is that they smile so frequently; dozens of times each day, according to one study. In adulthood, however, most people average about four smiles a day. What a loss! We need to join the *Share-A-Smile* club!

An unknown writer penned these words:

A smile, they tell us, is a curve that straightens out a lot of things.
So try one often, just to see how many blessings that it brings.

Wearing pleasant facial expressions most of the time does not mean we deny other appropriate emotions and feelings. It does mean that we recognize that approximately twenty percent of the affect to our lives from a given situation results from the event itself; eighty percent can be contributed by our perception of or response to the event. As mentioned in *BACK TO BASICS*, learning to identify, experience, and manage our emotions and feelings appropriately will help to create pleasing patterns in the fountains of our lives.

Some individuals find it very helpful to think of the range of emotions and feelings as a ladder. We want to spend as much time as possible at the rung of joy. However, we regularly move up and down the ladder as emotional flags signal us to pay attention to particular incidents in our lives. You may want to draw your own visual outline. Here is one example:

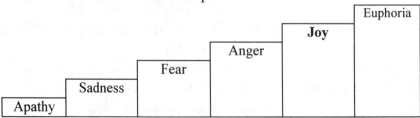

Aesthesia—Day Two

Table Nine—Problems related to aesthesia   Females—219 Males—102

	Never	Rarely	Sometimes	Frequently	Always
Females	5.0%	22.4%	45.6%	22.4%	4.6%
Males	3.0%	23.5%	44.1%	25.5%	3.9%
Overall	4.4%	22.7%	45.2%	23.3%	4.4%
Me					

Take a few moments to evaluate yourself:

- Am I honest with myself about my emotions/feelings?
- Are there certain emotions/feelings that I am willing to experience and others that I am not?
- Do I honor them while knowing that I do not have to act upon any of them or do I put them down?
- Is there some woundedness in my past that needs to be healed?
- Are there problems in my life related to my ability to manage my emotions and feelings appropriately?

Aesthesia—Day Three

Unmanaged emotions and feelings
add chaos, not color, to our lives. Anonymous

I am making a list of the events in my life that have contributed to my developing an ability to manage my emotions and feelings successfully. Likewise, I am listing the factors that influenced me to develop problems in the areas of emotions and feelings. I review the role-modeling I received in these areas. I look at these events and factors from a new perspective and I am learning from them. I treasure the positive and dispose of the negative. Today I trust my senses to give me valuable information. I understand that each emotion plays an important role in my life. I also understand that I control, to a large degree, the way in which they are translated into feelings. I have stopped disregarding my emotions and feelings. They are becoming valuable friends.

Aesthesia—Day Four

*Most of the mistakes in life come from _feeling_ when we
ought to think—and _thinking_ when we ought to feel. Anonymous*

All my emotions and feelings receive serious consideration. I
realize that I can experience all my feelings without choosing to act
upon any of them. Today I relate to my emotions and feelings as
flags that give me valuable information. I carefully and accurately
translate my emotions into feelings. I choose what I will feel, how
deeply I will feel, for how long I will maintain the feeling(s), and
whether or not I will act upon them. Managing my emotions and
feelings effectively frees me to *get on* with the process of thriving.
I choose to look at the behaviors of others and at all situations in
life as objectively as possible, rather than pretending there isn't a
need for improvement.

Aesthesia—Day Five

*We would not think of entering the home of our friends
and stealing their treasures; neither should we rob their lives
of happiness through our negative state of mind. Anonymous*

I am learning the difference between emotions and feelings;
between identifying and honoring them and acting them out.
Hiding, denying, or belittling any feeling is an act of disrespect. I
respect my own feelings as well as those of others. I refrain from
trying to tell others how they should feel. Today I honor all my
emotions and feelings and I respect others by acknowledging their
emotions and feelings. I do this without making any judgments. I
simply acknowledge. I am letting go of the negative feelings that I
have stored within my memory about a specific person or a
specific event from the past. I am relabeling yesterday's feelings as
just that, past feelings. I no longer fear experiencing the full range
of emotions and feelings available to me because I know that I
have the power to choose whether or not I will act upon them.

Aesthesia—Day Six

*The best and most beautiful things in the world cannot be seen
or even touched—they must be felt with the heart. Helen Keller*

I am treating myself as a kindly parent would treat a child. I recognize that when I have a hard time maintaining this approach, it's because of scars from less-than-optimal parenting and/or from abusive experiences earlier in life. Therefore, I am patiently reparenting myself in a way that I would like to have experienced during childhood. Today, I express affection for myself. This affection includes the nurturing of my physical body, my emotional and mental being, and my sexual and spiritual dimensions. As my self-esteem increases, my self-hate and inner conflict diminish and I no longer am motivated to binge on junk food or to diet excessively. I express respect toward myself through my high-level-wellness lifestyle. I am learning that I can choose to *feel* all my emotions and feelings—the entire exciting spectrum—without hanging on to them for ever and without acting on them. This is such an empowering position. I like it!

Aesthesia—Day Seven

*Rejoice with those who rejoice;
mourn with those who mourn. Romans 12:15*

I recognize that *moods* are often simply the result of an attempt to manage emotions intellectually without using the feeling function. I also realize that moods can become habit patterns. I can habitually exhibit so-called negative moods and become immobilized or destructive; I can exhibit false positive moods and ignore reality. Today I choose to be *real* in terms of owning my emotions and feelings. I also choose to continue my journey irrespective of any particular mood. I am in charge of me. I pay attention to my internal self-talk phrases related to emotions and feelings. When I recognize negative words that offer excuses for my failing to take responsibility for feelings and their related behaviors, I make a decision to change them. I am rehearsing new ways of talking about my emotions and feelings. These messages, containing my beliefs, are replayed continually whether or not I am consciously aware of them. They assist me in learning to manage my emotions and feelings effectively.

Aesthesia—Day Eight

Take on an entirely new way of life. Ephesians 4:23 (TM)

I am able to see beyond failures and mistakes, beyond uncomfortable encounters and situations, and can recognize the lesson to be learned. I look at a closed door as simply a flag to get me to look for the open door in another direction. I am no longer intimidated by obstacles but rejoice in the knowledge that there are no limits to my ability to discover and embrace the opportunity for renewal. A spoken word cannot be recalled; a harsh action cannot be undone. I am developing habits of emotional accord. I recognize my emotions, translate them as accurately as possible into feelings, and carefully select those that I will verbalize and/or act upon. Today I choose to associate with people who are positive and upbeat. In return, I choose to share positive, uplifting energy. This does not deny emotions of sadness, fear, and anger; it does mean that I choose not to remain morose and despairing.

Identify one specific behavior, related to the effective management of emotions and feelings, you are endeavoring to improve.

Aesthesia—Day Nine

List three specifics you have learned about yourself in relation to emotions and feelings.

- _____

  _____

- _____

  _____

- _____

  _____

Aesthesia—Day Ten

Learning to appropriately manage your emotions and feelings is empowering. Write down your personal affirmation related to emotions and feelings.

_____

_____

_____

_____

_____

_____

SHAME

CHAPTER TEN
MANAGING SHAME

Shame—Day One

Synonyms: Embarrassment, humiliation, dishonor

Antonym: Honor

The power of *interruption* usually develops by the age of eighteen months and onward as we absorb the mores of our family, church, and society. Shame momentarily interrupts whatever is going on so we can take stock and reassess. It is often evidenced by changes such as blushing, becoming temporarily tongue-tied, or experiencing an acute sense of discomfort.

Healthy shame enables us to recognize when we have made a mistake, when we have violated a law, an expectation or a rule of conduct. It tells us that we are human and that we can learn another way. Unhealthy or false shame is a sense that we *are* a mistake and can never learn a new way of behavior. False shame promotes feelings of hopelessness, helplessness, and inadequacy. It can totally immobilize us. Our task is to learn the difference between healthy shame and false shame; to learn to manage healthy shame appropriately; to avoid allowing false shame to manage us.

Babette was unable to enjoy a fulfilling sexual relationship with her husband because, as a child, she had been taught that sexual activity was bad, dirty, unmentionable—and should be saved for the person she loved the most (a husband). Much to the dismay of both parties, the wedding ceremony had not automatically erased this subconsciously absorbed attitude and the resulting unhealthy shame. Babette actually felt guilty for engaging in behaviors that were designed to promote joy and intimacy between her and her husband. Needless to say, this put a major strain on their marriage.

In his hurry to leave work for the ball game, Jerod printed out two letters for his supervisor without computer spell-checking them. The next morning, the letters were back on his desk with these words written in the margin in red ink: "Spelling errors.

Retype!" Jerod felt his face flush with healthy shame. Fortunately, he quickly realized that he could learn a *new way*. From now on, he would consistently utilize his computer's spell-check function.

Harriet was struggling with shame-by-association. While they were attending an adult education forum, her escort had disrupted the program with inappropriate comments. Later on, when a close friend invited Harriet to another presentation in the series, she hesitated for fear of what people might think of her. Fortunately, her friend helped Harriet to realize that she could not take responsibility for the behaviors of another adult. She need not allow false shame to cause her extended anguish or to limit her options.

We can begin to reorganize this facet of our lives by examining the beliefs and attitudes, concerning shame, we absorbed during childhood. Some of them may still be valid in adulthood; others may need to be revised; still others may need to be discarded altogether and be replaced with new ones.

We can internalize the difference between healthy shame and unhealthy shame, between healthy guilt and false guilt. Whenever we recognize feelings of shame (or guilt) we can make time—later that day or week if it is not possible to do so at the moment—to identify and label the feelings. We can make a conscious effort to connect them with a belief or an attitude and analyze whether or not we want to continue in the same pattern.

If the answer is yes, fine; if the answer is no, then we understand that we need to work on revising one or more of our beliefs and attitudes that trigger the shame or guilt in this case. By changing the way we *think* (our beliefs and attitudes) we will change the way we *feel* (in terms of the shame and guilt that is triggered in our lives).

False shame is a tiny
stream of fear,
Trickling through the mind.
If encouraged,
It cuts a channel
Into which all other thoughts
are drained.

Shame—Day Two

Table Ten—Problems related to shame   Females—219 Males—102

	Never	Rarely	Sometimes	Frequently	Always
Females	14.2%	38.4%	32.4%	12.3%	2.7%
Males	15.7%	36.3%	29.4%	15.7%	2.9%
Overall	14.6%	37.7%	31.5%	13.4%	2.8%
Me					

Take a few moments to evaluate yourself:

- Do I readily recognize mistakes for what they are; learning experiences that can lead to new choices?
- Do I beat myself up whenever I make a mistake, telling myself that I am a mistake and can never succeed?
- Are there problems in my life related to the way I handle shame?

Shame—Day Three

*Most of our unhappiness is the result
of comparing ourselves to others. Cherney*

I realize that without insight, derived from looking at my childhood through adult eyes, I am prone to repeat my generational history. Today I begin to list common behavioral patterns that run through my family-of-origin. Some of those behaviors I want to keep in my life; others I want to change or discard. I choose to break the cycle of unhealthy shame so that those who come after me will have less to unlearn. I am making a list of the events in my life that have contributed to my developing my present thought patterns and beliefs about shame. I am listing the factors that influenced me to develop problems with shame, especially in the area of unhealthy shame and false guilt. I look at these events and factors from a new perspective and I am learning from them. I retain the positive and dispatch the negative. Although I make mistakes, I myself am not a mistake.

Shame—Day Four

*Where there is shame,
there is hope for virtue. German Proverb*

I acknowledge the place that healthy shame plays in my life. It alerts me when I am breaching a code of ethics or of etiquette. Because it momentarily interrupts my activity, it gives me a chance to take a deep breath, evaluate what is going on inside and outside of me, and choose to take action as necessary. Today I understand that my beliefs about shame developed in my family-of-origin. I am releasing the negative beliefs/attitudes. Healthy shame gives me a chance to *course-correct* when necessary. Because I am giving up unhealthy shame and false guilt, I no longer fear shame; it no longer means that I am a bad person. I actually now welcome the input and use it to my advantage.

Shame—Day Five

*Sometimes the mistakes that slow
you down also save your life! Lawrence*

As I develop hope and trust, my Higher Power helps me to clear from my memory the accumulated shame from the past. I am living a renewed life with a new thinking style and new goals. Today my path includes forgiving the blunders of my past, making amends where possible, and living free of *unhealthy shame*. I think of shame as a *thermostat* that helps me stay balanced. When it momentarily interrupts my activities or my thoughts it gives me an opportunity to monitor them. I make the choice to continue *as is* or to pursue a different course. I am learning to separate healthy shame from the false shame that others may try to place upon me inappropriately. False shame is false logic because no failure (or success) is necessarily final. My spirit is resilient. I am learning a new way of thinking.

Shame—Day Six

*I have learned more from my mistakes
than I ever have from my successes. Taylor*

I accept my humanity. Because of it, I will make mistakes. Today I no longer see my mistakes as *shameful* but as positive learning opportunities. This perspective frees me from a great deal of false shame and guilt. I now look at my mistakes as stepping-stones rather than mountains of shame. Mistakes help me to know when to alter my behavioral patterns. I don't intentionally plan to make mistakes; I do plan to advantageously learn from them when they occur. I feel like my own *Sherlock Holmes* in this process and I enjoy the discoveries. I honor my past even as I honor my present. I am who I am because of everything I have experienced—and I like who I am.

Shame—Day Seven

*I set my face like flint and I know
I will not be put to shame. Isaiah 50:7*

The words *shame on you* are no longer part of my everyday vocabulary. The strident remarks and accusatory comments of others have less power over me. I am neither swayed by them nor diminished in self and spirit. I hear them but do not allow them to turn me aside from my journey nor to discourage me in my progress. I understand their comments are more about *them* than they are about *me*. Today I remove such remarks from my vocabulary—from the vocabulary I use with myself and with others—words like *should have, shouldn't have, could have, ah-ha!* I endeavor to extend an encircling aura of affirmation to myself and to others. I listen to and evaluate my internal self-talk tapes related to healthy and unhealthy shame. My revised thoughts are helping me to understand and manage shame appropriately. I utilize healthy shame as the useful tool it is. But I let go of it quickly and hold my head high in confidence. False shame is retreating altogether.

Shame—Day Eight

*The one who wins honors through a neighbor's
shame will never reach Paradise. Hebrew Proverb*

Mistakes are simply part of my learning process. Erasers on pencils serve to remind me that I can always try again. I can learn from my mistakes and revise my habit patterns. Today there are no failures in my life; simply events and situations from which I can learn. I repeat to myself: there are no failures—just a pause now and then to allow me to evaluate my behavior. I can try again and again. It is always my choice. I understand the benefits that derive from the judicious use of healthy shame. I also understand how unhealthy shame can destroy me. I appreciate this knowledge and incorporate it into my life. I give up false shame and allow healthy shame to enable me to select new options as necessary.

Identify one specific behavior, in relation to shame, that you are striving to improve.

_____

_____

_____

_____

_____

_____

Shame—Day Nine

List three things you have learned about yourself in relation to shame.

- _____

  _____

- _____

  _____

- _____

  _____

Shame—Day Ten

Good work! Internalizing the difference between healthy shame and false shame takes concerted effort. Write down your personal affirmation related to shame.

_____

_____

_____

_____

_____

_____

INDUSTRY

CHAPTER ELEVEN
PROMULGATING INDUSTRY

Industry—Day One

Synonyms: Diligence, perseverance, work

Antonym: Indolence

The power to accomplish is a developmental task ideally learned between the ages of six through eleven and then honed thereafter. Learning this task enables us to develop the ability to contribute positively and consistently throughout each day of our lives. We develop a sense of being able to realize worthwhile goals that can bring pleasure to ourselves as well as to others.

If we failed to develop industry, as adults we may follow the way of least resistance. We may be unable to hold down a responsible job or contribute appropriately in almost any type of relationship or situation. A lack of industry can lead to laziness as well as to a sense of inadequacy and inferiority.

One of my most treasured memories from childhood is that of my mother reading aloud. Her voice inflections are etched in my memory along with many of the lessons portrayed through the stories. One in particular was about seven boys who saw a large sign in the window of Hardwick's Hardware advertising a part-time position. Jobs were scarce and all seven decided to apply. They joked about who would get the job. Each boy was given an appointment and told that the interview would consist of organizing a trunk filled with old nuts, bolts, nails and washers.

After thinking it over, several of the boys withdrew their applications; others didn't bother to return. Tony showed up for his interview and spent five hours industriously sorting and labeling the contents of the old trunk. Near the bottom he discovered a small white card. It read, "Congratulations. If you have gotten this far, you have the job. Bring this card to the office." The card was signed, Mr. Hardwick. Tony's ability to be industrious earned him the coveted position.

Reports by returned POWs indicate that deliberate mental rehearsal (a form of industry) helped to keep them sane and centered during years of imprisonment. They honed their ability to actively create internal pictures. This skill enabled them to plan inventions, practice music, write poetry, recall memorization, rehearse solutions to mathematical problems and engage in a host of other mental gymnastics. In a similar way we can develop the art of mental rehearsal, an activity that can enable us to remain centered even in the midst of chaos.

We can self-assess by carefully uncovering factors within our family-of-origin that might have contributed to our lack of industry. Some of us grew up with a model of unemployment; some with seasonal employment only; some with workaholism. For some, education was not emphasized; for others it was touted as the only ladder to success.

We can also honestly evaluate our tendency toward procrastination. Human beings often procrastinate tasks that require functions directed by their non-preferent brain quadrants. Understanding this tendency can encourage us to make conscious choices about developing industry. For example, we can:

- take positive steps toward developing the competencies (skills honed by practice) we need to be successful
- team up with others who have strengths in our areas of weakness
- *course correct* when we have been adapting away from our innate giftedness
- take responsibility for breaking habits of procrastination and developing new patterns of industry.

It is important to structure our lives to allow sufficient time for necessary accomplishments. We can learn to enjoy the sense of mastery that accrues as we positively contribute to our own lives and to the lives of those around us in a systematic manner. Tasks look less formidable when we divide them into individual steps. When we approach them from a one-at-a-time perspective, it is often amazing how much we can easily accomplish.

A little poem, written by Kathleen Cafferky Taylor, underscores this philosophy. It is entitled, *One By One.*

It's one at a time, just one by one,
Over and over till the task is done.

One stitch at a time and the trousers are mended,
One stride at a time and the long race is ended.

One chip at a time and the big tree will fall,
One brick at a time will build the strong wall.

One stick at a time and you'll pile up the wood,
One weed at a time and the garden looks good.

With many a rub the car will shine,
And a book is soon read if you go line by line.

You'll not be discouraged when work's to be done,
If you will remember to work *one by one.*

Industry—Day Two

Table Eleven—Problems related to industry   Females—219 Males—102

	Never	Rarely	Sometimes	Frequently	Always
Females	23.7%	45.2%	22.4%	5.5%	3.2%
Males	25.5%	38.2%	19.6%	13.7%	3.0%
Overall	24.3%	43.0%	21.5%	8.1%	3.1%
Me					

Take a few moments to evaluate yourself:

- Do I sense a laziness within myself that holds me back from contributing positively in life?
- Can I identify specific tasks that I try to avoid?
- Am I willing to collaborate with others when to do so would improve the outcomes?
- Is procrastination a barrier to my success?
- Do I have problems related to industry?

Industry—Day Three

Be very careful then, how you live—not as unwise but
as wise, making the most of every opportunity. Ephesians 5:15-16

I am making a list of the events in my life that have contributed to my developing the ability to accomplish that which I choose to undertake. Likewise I am listing the factors that influenced me to develop problems in the area of accomplishment. I am looking at these events and factors from a new perspective and I am learning from them. I keep both lists for handy reference. Today, I am willing to look at areas that need growth and behavioral changes. I am deleting the word *procrastination* from my vocabulary and the behavior from my life. I choose to begin making the most of every opportunity—now. What I do (or don't do) today, has a profound effect on my life tomorrow. I am learning to recall yesterday, live in the present, and plan for the future. It is easier than I once thought possible!

Industry—Day Four

Yesterday is gone, tomorrow has not yet
arrived, make the most of today. Old Proverb

I dream my dreams knowing that the future has much in store for me. I use my time diligently to accomplish necessary tasks. Today I am careful how I live. I take steps toward my dreams, building on the stepping-stones that I have already developed. I choose to <u>try</u>. When something does not work out exactly as I envisioned it I do not use the word failure. I simply chalk it up as another learning experience. I compliment my effort—and look for another way. I know that disappointment is simply a state of mind and I can develop a different perspective. Interestingly enough, with my new outlook, I am experiencing fewer failures. I make the most of every day. This approach is rapidly becoming a user-friendly habit.

Industry—Day Five

Don't just do what you have to do to get by, but work heartily...and work with a smile on your face. Ephesians 6:6 (TM)

I am endeavoring to stay in tune with my Higher Power. I am gradually learning to pay attention to that still small voice within me. My heart longs to be made willing. Today I work sincerely and industriously. I am learning to avoid the way of least resistance, to give up habits of procrastination. I am organizing my life, learning to manage it more effectively. This is resulting in a diminished sense of scarcity. There is plenty of time for accomplishment and for nurturing, plenty of time for myself and for my family-of-choice, plenty of time for recovery—heartfelt recovery, plenty of time for sharing with others. When I work from the heart, my life seems to unfold much more smoothly. In fact, I like the thought that I am part of a master plan.

Industry—Day Six

Whatever your hand finds to do, do it with all your might. Ecclesiastes 9:10

Many times in the past I failed to even begin because I did not have a clear picture of my goals. Now I know that it is not only important to have personal goals, it is important to keep my dreams alive. Accomplishment and success are not achieved by wishing someone else would start the project. I nurture the spark within me that keeps my dreams alive and well. Today I make time to reaffirm my aspirations. I see each one of them in my thoughts and explore them thoroughly as they are projected on the drawing board of my imagination. I begin my own projects, oil the works, and see them successfully executed. I use my *elbow grease* to get the machinery of success in my life running smoothly. I discipline myself to be industrious. I am becoming the best I can be with all my might. This is the most important journey I will ever take, so I'm giving it all I've got!

Industry—Day Seven

*No one can do everything but
everyone can do something. Old Adage*

I realize that I cannot do everything but I can develop the skills of discipline and industry. I can do this well. I am carefully listening to my internal self-talk tapes about industry, paying attention to what I hear. I evaluate each phrase for its potential to nurture and affirm me or to discourage and sabotage. When I recognize a negative phrase that would derail industry, I make a decision to change it. I *turn down* the volume on old, unhelpful messages and concentrate instead on recording new, positive self-talk messages. I am rehearsing thoughts and words that help me to improve the skill of industry. These helpful messages are replayed continually whether or not I am consciously aware of them; they positively influence my thoughts and my behaviors.

Industry—Day Eight

*Go to the ant...consider its ways and be wise. It has no
commander, no overseer or ruler, yet it stores its provisions
in summer and gathers its food at harvest. Proverbs 6:6*

Like the ant I am self-motivated. I *store* provisions, as it were, through my recovery work. Today I welcome my tasks. I feel alive and sense myself progressing. There is no substitute for industry. I no longer side-step work; it has become a trusted friend. Already I see the harvest that I am reaping. My food is the success that I am achieving, the growth that is being accomplished within me. I am inspired by the beauty and complexity of nature, by the beauty and complexity of life, by the beauty and complexity of my journey.

Identify one specific behavior, in relation to industry, that you have targeted for improvement.

Industry—Day Nine

List three personal discoveries in relation to industry.

* _____

_____

* _____

_____

* _____

_____

Industry—Day Ten

It's wonderful to be able to utilize the power of accomplishment on a daily basis. Write down your personal affirmation related to industry.

_____

_____

_____

_____

_____

_____

_____

COMPETENCE

CHAPTER TWELVE
AUGMENTING COMPETENCE

Competence—Day One

Synonyms: Adequacy, capability, expertise

Antonym: Incompetence

The power of adequacy is the developmental task paired with industry. Learning competence enables us to develop a sense of capability sufficient to handle the necessities and vicissitudes of life. We understand the difference between the temporal trap of perfectionism (trying to perform every activity flawlessly) and the ethic of perfection (being well-suited for the task at hand and doing our best with the resources available to us).

If we did not learn competence, as adults we may be unable to evaluate personal performance realistically or at all. We may thus be handicapped in acquiring the wherewithal to obtain the necessities of life. We may be unable to compete successfully in the marketplace and may needlessly expend energy striving for *perfectionism*—an unrealistic mind-set that can cause burnout and adversely affect all our efforts and relationships.

The ability to be persistent can help us to achieve competence. Laura could often be heard to remark, "If at first you don't succeed, try, try again."

How different from Belle, who frequently stood apart from others at social gatherings, looking like a wallflower—albeit a very attractive wallflower. During a school picnic, Belle repeatedly refused all invitations to take part in the activities. "I'm not very good at games," she murmured.

After hearing yet another refusal to participate, an older woman standing near Belle said encouragingly, "Practice makes perfect. Go ahead and try. You will get good at it eventually." "

But if I don't try, then I can't fail," Belle responded. "

I guess that depends upon your definition of failure," the woman answered. "In my book, not *trying* is failure."

Alice was having a dreadful experience in driving school. She could not stay in her lane or turn corners smoothly. Finally, in frustration, the driving instructor asked somewhat impatiently, "How did you ever manage riding a bike?"

"I never learned to ride a bike," Alice replied. The instructor promptly sent her home to spend some time learning to ride a bike. When she became competent in that skill, she was to return to class and resume driving school. It worked. The competence Alice developed on a bicycle enabled her to successfully obtain her driver's license.

We must *realistically* define a standard of competence and then aim for it consistently. What is right for us will not necessarily be right for others and vice versa. There may also be different levels of competence within our lives for different types of activities. For example, we may choose to spend longer hours developing competence on our musical instrument of choice and less time honing proficiency in the game of tennis that we enjoy occasionally.

We need to take stock of our innate strengths and weaknesses; building on our strengths and striving to improve in areas of weakness. We will usually develop a higher level of competence in areas in which we are gifted—and we are all gifted in one way or another!

Identifying our strengths and weaknesses can serve as a baseline for making decisions about areas in which we need to grow. It can also help us to make conscious choices about collaborating with others who possess strengths in our areas of weakness. We each have areas in which we need to improve. We each have something to learn from others. We each have something that we can share with others. Collectively we can achieve a greater whole.

Competence—Day Two

Table Twelve—Problems related to competence   Females—216 Males—102

	Never	Rarely	Sometimes	Frequently	Always
Females	13.9%	42.6%	31.0%	9.7%	2.8%
Males	19.6%	38.2%	20.6%	13.7%	7.9%
Overall	15.7%	41.2%	27.7%	11.0%	4.4%
Me					

Take a few moments to evaluate yourself:

- Do I usually feel inadequate and fail to follow through on tasks ?
- Do I feel competent most of the time, looking at my personal performance realistically and accepting myself and my efforts even when the task is not completed perfectly?
- Are there problems in my life related to my competence?

Competence—Day Three

*Instead of looking for guarantees
in life, look for choices. Unknown*

I am making a list of the events in my life that have contributed to my perception of my own adequacy and to the standards for competence that I embrace. Likewise I am listing the factors that influenced me to develop problems in the areas of adequacy and competence. I am looking at these events and factors from a new perspective and I am learning from them. I am keeping my eyes open for positive factors that I can add on a daily basis. Today, I do not wait for something external to happen that will help me to feel more competent. I simply move forward with confidence, unsticking myself from comfortable plateaus of lethargy. I possess both strength and energy. I am using that strength and energy to carry through the projects that I have chosen and to complete them competently. I understand the difference between competency and perfection and I am achieving balance in this area of my life.

Competence—Day Four

Those who are skilled in
work will serve before kings. Old Proverb

My strengths are built-in and I am learning to recognize and value them. Today I realize that *God don't make no junk!* I have confidence in my ability to develop competence. I am facing my problems, adversities, and confusions with assurance. I feel my inner strength—and I am empowered. I am learning the difference between showing off and really excelling. I compliment myself for developing the ability to be competent. I have written down specific situations in which I have exhibited the power of adequacy. My list is growing. I nurture myself for the progress I am making. I am choosing to be the type of person who makes things happen. My life is steadily improving day by day because of this choice.

Competence—Day Five

The best preparation for tomorrow is to
do today's work superbly well. Sir William Osler

I may march to a different drummer but I must march to the beat I hear. Sometimes this means that I am all alone on the parade route. I feel okay to be alone in my endeavor some of the time. It is important for me to follow the beat of my own drum, to continue the course I have set upon, to nurture the need I see unfulfilled. Today, I am trusting my instincts even though others may think differently. I listen to their suggestions and honor my convictions. I do not fear. My soul reverberates with resolution. I am developing strength. I actually feel stronger. As my track record improves in the area of adequacy, my episodes of fear diminish. I believe that the growth I am making right now will serve me well in the days and years to come.

Competence—Day Six

The wise are able to learn from the
mistakes of others as well as their own. Cherney

I am learning to feel more competent moment by moment as I walk the journey of life. I realize that it is not enough to simply read what others have said about competence, I need to take that journey myself. Today I live my life with confidence. I know that tomorrow I will again walk confidently into the future. I have more energy because I am not wasting it on fearful, anxious thoughts and behaviors. I do what I can today and plan for tomorrow. I am learning from my mistakes; I am profiting not only from my experience but from the experiences of others. I can learn some lessons through observation. As I heal, I am discovering the gift of laughter. It lightens my heart and helps me to note and celebrate each newly-gained skill.

Competence—Day Seven

We are what we repeatedly do.
Excellence, then, is not an act, but a habit. Aristotle

I round another corner in life and am amazed at who I was intended to be. Today I take an additional step in my journey. I am excited by the open doors that reveal incredible opportunities; opportunities I might not even have recognized in the past. I like myself. I enjoy seeing the real me unfold and mature. Each new step brings a new perspective that excites me. Discovering who I am and honing competencies is hard work. I choose to invest the necessary time and energy, however. It is the most rewarding investment I have ever made. The returns are exponential! I am carefully listening to my internal self-talk tapes about competence. When I recognize a negative unhelpful phrase, I make a decision to change it. I am rehearsing thoughts and words that help me to improve my competence. These messages are replayed continually whether or not I am consciously aware of them. They are helping me to feel more competent and to actually become more competent.

Competence—Day Eight

Bragging is the veneer of the incompetent. Ancient Proverb

I am learning the difference between *bragging* and acknowledging my progress. I reward myself for each new sprig of competence. I have written down tasks in which I have become competent. My list is getting longer. I no longer put myself down when I make mistakes. Rather, I nurture myself for the progress I am making. It is fun to look into the mirror and tell myself, "You are doing a good job." I mean the words honestly and know that they are true. As my level of competence improves, so does my sense of self-worth. I do feel better about myself as I perceive my adequacy increasing. However, my level of self-worth is largely independent of my competence.

Identify one specific behavior, in relation to competence, that you are striving to improve.

_____

_____

Competence—Day Nine

List three qualities of your competence.

- _____

_____

- _____

_____

- _____

_____

Competence—Day Ten

Congratulate yourself. Write down your personal affirmation related to competence.

_____

_____

_____

_____

_____

_____

_____

_____

_____

_____

_____

_____

GENDER IDENTITY

CHAPTER THIRTEEN
VALIDATING GENDER IDENTITY

Gender Identity—Day One

Synonyms: Male or female

Antonym: Hermaphrodite

The power of accepting and respecting our *core gender identity* is a developmental task that often begins even before our birth. Human beings possess a core gender identity of being either male or female. We accept and respect that core identity based on what we hear people say about gender, how we are treated individually, and what we see in terms of the way in which others are treated.

In general, society is gender-biased, often overtly or subtly rewarding one gender over the other in terms of opportunity, compensation, and career advancement. In addition, some families give their children the message that one gender is preferred. At times, children may even perceive that they were unwanted because of their particular gender.

As children, if we perceived that our gender was equally valued and respected, we likely learned to extend that sense of value to ourselves as well as to others. If the opposite was true, as adults we may approach life from either a one-up or a one-down position—neither of which promotes functional, equalitarian relationships.

During childhood, Danny was encouraged to be assertive and was consistently offered opportunities that were denied Darla, his twin. As a result, both children absorbed the belief that boys were better than girls, a perception that influenced every facet of their lives. Darla came to resent the fact that she had been born female and used this as an excuse for mediocrity. Danny approached his career activities more confidently but consistently exhibited offender behaviors toward females.

As a single parent, Ken's mother was concerned that his being raised in a family with three sisters might not provide sufficient male role-modeling. She recognized that he needed to spend time with an appropriate male role-model. Accordingly, she made the necessary arrangements. Her actions can enable Ken to accept and respect his core gender identity in a way that might not otherwise have been possible.

Respecting gender identity means valuing individuals for their innate strengths and for their personal choices regardless of whether or not their behaviors conform to our perceptions of appropriateness. More and more we see individuals stepping outside of the stereotypical roles that once were overemphasized by our culture. Stephanie enjoys her career as a forest ranger; Dillon thrives as a bedside nurse in a convalescent hospital. Jillian and Eric enjoy what some would call a reversed-role marriage in terms of traditional expectations. Jillian is a courtroom attorney; Eric is a househusband. They each excel in their roles and their partnership is highly successful. We applaud them all.

We need to understand the value that our Higher Power places upon human beings regardless of gender. We must learn to positively regard each gender as equal although different, understanding that the word different means unlike and does not imply unequal. We need to resist any temptation to hold one gender to a higher standard.

Many children grew up hearing rhymes such as:

What are little boys made of?
Snips and snails and puppy-dog tails.
What are little girls made of?
Sugar and spice and all things nice.

These may be *cute* verses but what messages do they give children? It is important to evaluate the words we use and delete those that evidence a negative gender bias (e.g., slut, stud, broad, wolf, old bat, sleaze bag). Moving toward gender-inclusiveness in language can promote the validation of gender identity.

We need to value ourselves and others simply because we exist, understanding that even though we did not choose our core identity, we can respect and appreciate it. If we truly accept and honor our own gender identity, we will be more likely to accept and honor that of others.

Gender Identity—Day Two

Table Thirteen—Gender-identity problems   Females—218 Males—102

	Never	Rarely	Sometimes	Frequently	Always
Females	60.5%	20.6%	9.6%	4.6%	4.6%
Males	64.7%	14.7%	5.9%	7.8%	6.9%
Overall	61.9%	18.8%	8.4%	5.6%	5.3%
Me					

Take a few moments to evaluate yourself:

- Do I believe that my gender is equally valued?
- Am I clear about my personal gender identity?
- Do I wish that I had been born the opposite gender?
- Do I use gender-inclusive language?
- Are there problems in my life related to gender identity?

Gender Identity—Day Three

...male and female He created them. Genesis 1:27

I am making a list of the events in my life that have contributed to my developing respect for my own gender. Likewise, I am listing the factors that have influenced me to develop problems in the area of gender identification. I look at these events and factors from a new perspective and I am learning from them. I nurture the positive and delete the negative. Today I concentrate on developing clarity in terms of gender identification. I respect who I am. I appreciate my own gender and I role-model respect for both genders. I understand that I need to make choices that are right for me; this is my responsibility. It is not my responsibility to make choices for other adults. I am also becoming more aware of the words I use. Each day I have the opportunity to make more functional choices and I am moving toward exhibiting gender-inclusive language.

Gender Identity—Day Four

Let each think of oneself as an act of God. Old Saying

Perceiving myself as a deliberate creation rather than as simply an accident of history helps me to value myself. Human beings are valuable. My Higher Power values each one, values me as a member of my gender. I choose to prevent my inner conflict from exhibiting itself as disrespect for my own gender. Today I recognize that as a member of my gender, I possess feminine and masculine energies within myself. Everyone does. I accept that fact with all its complexity. I do not use my body and my gender as a battleground for my as-yet-unresolved conflicts. I accept, affirm, enjoy, and care for my body as a valuable representative of my gender. I am developing a routine for decision making related to my personal gender identity. I calmly and clearly quiet my thoughts and evaluate the pros and cons. I feel neither overwhelmed nor rushed. There is little anxiety in this process because I have the freedom to make a different decision about any issue if evidence points to that need. This knowledge helps to reduce indecision.

Gender Identity—Day Five

Among us you are all equal. Galatians 3:28 (TM)

My Higher Power assigns equal value to both genders. This helps me to avoid perceiving myself as a victim or to exhibit offender behaviors based on gender identification. Today I am choosing to neither overvalue nor undervalue individuals based upon gender— regardless of stereotypical expectations from society, family, friends, church, club, career, or organization. I am increasing my knowledge of the innate differences between the genders, realizing that we are more alike than we are different. Some of my frustrations are diminishing as I understand more about gender differences. My goal is not to minimize or to exaggerate the differences, but simply to understand them, accept them, and appreciate them.

Gender Identity—Day Six

*What you possess in this world will go to someone else
when you die, but what you are will be yours forever. Proverb*

I am giving up all pseudo fear related to my own gender. I am OK and can act fearlessly on my own behalf. I view myself as apart from and yet part of all. There is not another human being anywhere that is exactly *me*. I bear a distinct individuality and can impact the universe in a way that would be missed were I not in existence. Today I am learning to know who I am, a prototype of my gender. I understand that the concept of accepting and respecting my core sexual identity as a human being is separate from exhibiting sexual activity. I am careful of the words I use in connection with gender. Today I understand that I can own my gender and feel all the feelings related to sexuality without acting upon any of them. I make discriminating choices related to my sexual being and to my sexual behaviors.

Gender Identity—Day Seven

I am fearfully and wonderfully made. Psalm 139:14

I am carefully listening to the messages that play inside my head about the value of my own gender. I pay attention to what I hear and evaluate each phrase for its potential to improve the respect I have for each gender or to tear down. When I recognize a negative phrase that puts down gender (mine or that of another) I make a decision to change it. I turn down the volume on those stereotypical and dysfunctional messages. I concentrate instead on recording new, positive self-talk messages that honor both genders. I am rehearsing thoughts and words that help me to build a healthy respect for my own gender identity. These messages are replayed continually whether or not I am consciously aware of them. They influence how highly I respect myself for who I am at my very core. Today I recognize that I am fearfully and wonderfully made. It is an awesome recognition!

Gender Identity—Day Eight

Practice in decision-making today
makes one stronger for the morrow. Lawrence

I am feeling more and more comfortable with my gender identity. I know who I am and like who I am. Challenges to my gender identity no longer present a threat. In fact, I am constantly facing challenges and am constantly growing stronger as a member of my gender. When I encounter a new challenge or a new person I feel less awkward; I simply call upon my past experience to assist me in making a decision. Once I have made my decision it is not cast in concrete. As new information becomes available, I am able to change my decision or to change a portion of my decision. This ability relieves me of the overwhelming pressure of having to *make the right decision* immediately, in every situation. Today I am learning to be more direct in dealing with myself and others. I do this kindly and nonabrasively—and I do it! I ask myself pointedly about my goals and dreams. I ask others for help. I do not always receive exactly what I ask for but I have a much better shot at it when I know what I need and can articulate it. This is life. I am glad that I am part of it.

Identify one specific behavior, in relation to accepting and respecting your core identity, that you are striving to improve.

_____

_____

_____

_____

_____

_____

Gender Identity—Day Nine

List three things you have learned in relation to gender identity.

- _____

  _____

- _____

  _____

- _____

  _____

Gender Identity—Day Ten

Keep on making strides in accepting and respecting your core identity. Write your personal affirmation related to gender identity.

_____

_____

_____

_____

_____

_____

_____

IMAGINING

CHAPTER FOURTEEN
ENCOURAGING IMAGINING

Imagining—Day One

Synonyms: Conceptualizing, conceiving, creating, envisioning

Antonym: Nonconceptualizing

The power of *active mental picturing* is a developmental task that comes into its own as the right frontal lobe of the brain matures. Learning to imagine enables us to create internal pictures of something that is not present at the moment, of inventions that have not yet been developed, of ideas that can blossom in the future.

If we did not learn to imagine, we may become satisfied with the status quo, may be unable to envision a better life, may be stuck following only the ideas of others, may fail to step outside of the bounds passed down to us generationally. If we learned to imagine inappropriately we may be at risk for worrying excessively about the past or obsessing anxiously about the future. We may even develop compulsive behaviors related to our obsessive thoughts.

Unfortunately, much of today's favored entertainment generally enhances passive picturing rather than active picturing. Laureen, a middle-school teacher, could quickly identify the students who watched TV or played computer games a great deal of the time. During free time in the classroom or on the playground, they were unable to occupy their time creatively. Instead, they were likely to lament, "There isn't anything to do." How different from two students whose parents carefully monitored their TV/computer game time. These children were full of ideas, able to amuse themselves, and were seldom bored. Little wonder that they quickly became leaders in their class.

If we find that the power of active picturing is somewhat lacking in our lives—or virtually undeveloped—we can begin by limiting activities that encourage passive picturing (e.g., television, movies, videos, some computer games) and scheduling time every day for activities that promote *active* picturing (e.g., reading/telling/hearing stories, listening to personal growth tapes, developing hobbies, exchanging ideas with friends). Scheduling time for healthful and healing meditation can enhance our personal and spiritual growth, as well.

Maurice did not understand the difference between different forms of meditative imagining that he had heard discussed. He became involved with one form that encouraged him to *empty* his mind of all thought—a questionable practice considering the fact that the human brain was not designed to be empty of thought. Efforts to calm one's mental chaos and to carefully select one's thoughts represent an entirely different position from one that suggests a person try to avoid thinking. The mind will continue processing. Consequently, it is important to choose the thought(s) we wish to ponder.

Fortunately, a friend encouraged Maurice to practice the form of meditative imagining that advocates *filling* one's mind with a desired thought or idea and then quietly pondering it. He was almost amazed to discover how rapidly his recovery and personal growth journey improved as he internally pictured the new behaviors that he wanted to incorporate into his life and actually *saw in his mind's eye* the person he was becoming.

Imagining—Day Two

Table Fourteen—Problems with imagining   Females—208 Males—102

	Never	Rarely	Sometimes	Frequently	Always
Females	33.2%	37.0%	20.6%	6.3%	2.9%
Males	30.4%	32.4%	18.6%	14.7%	3.9%
Overall	32.3%	35.5%	20.0%	9.0%	3.2%
Me					

Take a few moments to evaluate yourself:

- Do I regularly schedule time to read, to meditate, to internally picture?
- How much time do I spend on activities that enhance active picturing versus passive picturing?
- Do I have problems related to imagining?

Imagining—Day Three

Be transformed by the renewing of your mind. Romans 12:2

I am making a list of the events and factors in my life that have contributed to my present habits related to imagining. I am looking at these events and factors from a new perspective and I am learning from them. I retain the positive and erase the negative. I understand that my mind was created with the ability to actively create internal mental pictures. Today I am using that brain function to see myself as the person I am becoming. That picture is becoming clearer. Now I chuckle whenever I hear someone say, "There's nothing to do." I know that there is always something for me to do. I carry my internal pictures with me. I can look at them whenever and wherever I choose. They help me to remain centered even when there is chaos on every side. I savor this developing ability. Practice reinforces intention and I awake every morning with hope in my heart. This helps me to expect that my journey today will go well. Whatever happens can work together for good.

Imagining—Day Four

Thought is the blossom, language
the bud, action the fruit behind it. Emerson

I am learning the difference between dysfunctional *magical thinking* and developing the ability to think realistically and creatively. I no longer fear imagining because I know that I am able to control it. In fact, it helps me harness the power to accomplish the goals that I have set. Today I combine active mental picturing with the ability to take action. I *see* a picture of something that heretofore I have never thought possible for myself. When I am tempted to become discouraged with my progress I remember that little by little, step by step, petal by petal it unfolds like a flower in my life. I am developing a skill that will endure through all the stages of my life. I am learning to picture the goals I expect to achieve as already accomplished and to move confidently toward the realization of those goals.

Imagining—Day Five

Very little is needed to make a happy life. It is all within yourself, in your way of thinking. Marcus Aurelius

Word pictures help me to develop the ability of imagination. I understand that happiness comes from within and that it follows my thoughts. I am learning to create internal pictures. These mental images make my personal and spiritual growth become much more real to me. When I picture *I can't,* I am usually right. The reverse is also true. When I imagine *I can,* I usually can! Today I picture positive outcomes. I use humor to remind myself that "all my dreams may not come true today but I am most thankful that my nightmares won't, either." I know that if I only look at what is, I may never attain what could be. I use my imagination to discover new options, to try another way, to learn a needful lesson, to look at a situation from a different perspective— to attain what can be.

Imagining—Day Six

A bird never soars too high when it soars with its own wings. Anonymous

I imagine that I am an eaglet on its initiation flight. I am making choices that fit me. I no longer automatically acquiesce to the expectations of others. Their ideas may be good but mine are right for me. Sometimes our perspectives match; sometimes they don't. When they don't, I am still able to maintain my flight. I have given up trying to be who others expect me to be. The price tag was too steep in terms of depression, physical illness, restlessness, unhappiness, and compulsive behaviors. Today I choose the recovery path to health and serenity. I have the energy and the incentive to carry my goals through to notable fruition. I choose to soar a little bit higher. The expanded view is great! I realize that what I accomplish in life depends to a great degree on what I imagine to be possible. My positive attitude is making a big difference in my life.

Imagining—Day Seven

Imagination is the highest kite one can fly. Lauren Bacall

Many times in my life I have delayed my progress waiting for just the *right time*. Today is the right time to develop the power of mental imaging. It is a pleasant journey, a rewarding way in which to live. I pay attention to my internal self-talk tapes about imagining, listening for the presence of phrases such as *day dreaming is a complete waste of time*. I evaluate each phrase for its potential to affirm and nurture my ability to imagine or to suppress it. When I recognize a negative phrase that puts down my ability to imagine, I make a decision to change it. I am rehearsing thoughts and words that help me to honor and expand my ability to conceptualize effectively. My ability to imagine successfully is improving by leaps and bounds.

Imagining—Day Eight

Stronger than all the armies in the world
is an idea whose time has come. Victor Hugo

Imagining helps me to look for the open door rather than pine over the closed one. When one door closes I simply expect that another one has already opened and I face in a different direction. There is always an open door. Sometimes it is not exactly the size, shape, or color that I expected—but one is always there. I am learning to recognize the open door more quickly. This practice helps me in other ways. I look for the silver lining behind each dark cloud, the sparkle in every raindrop, the happiness deep within my being. As my thinking becomes more positive and imaginative, I am a magnet for positive outcomes. I am encouraged. This is not a cat-and-mouse game; this is an exciting journey. I have stopped searching ineffectively; I have stopped banging my head against doors that have closed. I know what I need, am able to state those needs, and work to obtain them. I'm learning to recognize success even when it comes packaged slightly differently from what I expected. In fact, I like surprises!

Identify one specific behavior, in relation to imagining, that you are working to improve.

_____

_____

_____

_____

_____

_____

Imagining—Day Nine

List three things you have learned about yourself in relation to your skill of imagining.

- _____

_____

- _____

_____

- _____

_____

Imagining—Ten

Isn't it helpful to be able to picture in your *mind's eye* that which you are moving toward? Never underestimate the power of imagining! Use it wisely! Write down your personal affirmation related to imagining.

_____

_____

_____

_____

_____

_____

_____

_____

_____

_____

_____

_____

_____

INTEREST

CHAPTER FIFTEEN
FACILITATING INTEREST

Interest—Day One

Synonyms: Attention, attraction, curiosity

Antonyms: Boredom, apathy

The power of *attention* is a potential ability that is innately part of each undamaged human brain. It needs to be recognized and cultivated however. If we have developed a mind-set of interest, we possess a perpetual curiosity, a willingness to look at our world in a new way, a desire to learn, the ability to concentrate our attention for appropriate lengths of time.

If our attempts to satisfy our curiosity during childhood were met with ridicule or punishment, we may have learned to suppress this motivator. We may actually have developed habits of inattention or learned to avoid trying. As adults, we may respond to new information with fear, indifference, or outright rejection— before we have even spent time to evaluate it. We may exhibit a demeanor characterized by snobbery, apathy, or fear of the unknown. We may miss out on a great deal in life.

As soon as she could crawl, Victoria was a mobile question mark. She wanted to examine everything she saw, snails, tadpoles, worms, bugs, caterpillars, anything that moved. Her parents, however, expected her to be the stereotypical perfect little girl. They didn't like her to get her shoes scuffed, her hands dirty, her little dresses soiled. She repeatedly heard phrases such as, "Put that down. Girls shouldn't touch those. That's dirty. How icky! Be careful of germs." Gradually, Victoria stopped being interested in the world around her. As an adult, she endured life exhibiting only a modicum of enthusiasm. Although her parents frequently commented on her apathy, they never could seem to understand their contribution to its development.

At times our curiosity can lead us into trouble. Rick put his eye up to the knothole in the fence to see where all the bees were going. An annoyed bumble bee didn't appreciate this invasion of privacy and promptly stung Rick just below the eye. A sympathetic friend reminded Rick (somewhat tongue-in-cheek) that if he had been paying attention, he might have heard the bee humming a melody something like, "Be-e-e interested, be-e-e judicious, be-e-e ware."

We can begin to cultivate interest by choosing one particular subject to investigate; perhaps a topic we would like to have had the opportunity to explore in childhood. Remember, it is important to reward ourselves for exhibiting enthusiasm and interest as we progress. We may need to discard some of the old negative childhood tapes related to curiosity or at least turn down the volume on them. They are, after all, simply the opinions of other individuals and may no longer be valid in adulthood.

We need to consciously remain in a state of relaxed, interested alertness. That does sound like an oxymoron, but there is a huge difference between being consciously open to new information in a calm and deliberate manner and the frantic perpetual motion exhibited by individuals who are trying to dull the internal pain that has not been addressed and healed.

If you need some lessons on how to be curious, interested, and attentive simply go to a park or playground. Observe how little children respond with great interest to each other and to their environment. Notice how the smallest detail is often minutely examined. Smile, even chuckle, with their joy of discovery. Reclaim the child within you and encourage it to help you rediscover and develop interest. Someone has said: interest is what gets us started; the reward of discovery is what keeps us going.

> Life is full of such wonderful things,
> With vibrant surprise it always rings.
> Something different in ev'ry day,
> Makes it unique in a special way.
>
> Plan to love life and you soon will see,
> Wonderful things wherever you'll be.
> Even the common trifles will seem,
> In light of new attitudes—to gleam.

Interest—Day Two

Table Fifteen—Problems with interest   Females—219 Males—101

	Never	Rarely	Sometimes	Frequently	Always
Females	26.9%	45.2%	20.1%	4.6%	3.2%
Males	22.8%	40.5%	23.8%	9.9%	3.0%
Overall	25.6%	43.7%	21.3%	6.3%	3.1%
Me					

Take a few moments to evaluate yourself:

- Do I maintain an ongoing curiosity and pay attention to what is going on around me?
- Is my attention span long enough to enable me to complete my projects and achieve my goals?
- Are there problems in my life related to interest?

Interest—Day Three

Let the wise listen and add to their learning. Proverbs 1:5

I am making a list of the events in my life that have contributed to my ability to pay attention and to exhibit interest. Likewise I am listing the factors that influence my inattention and a lack of interest. I am looking at these events and factors from a new perspective and I am learning from them. I post both lists where they will get my attention on a daily basis. I hone the positive factors and purpose to revamp negative factors that persist in my life. I realize that, first of all, I have harmed myself and my personal growth through a lack of attention and curiosity. Today I am making amends to myself. I choose to focus my interest and my attention in areas that enhance my personal and spiritual growth. I am listening with interest: to myself, to others, to the environment. I am amazed at how this adds to my learning.

Interest—Day Four

Interest is to thriving what oxygen is to breathing. Cherney

My train of thought today determines my station in life tomorrow. I give myself the gift of attentive thinking. I choose to live with a mind-set of curiosity. Today I select one topic about which I know very little but in which I am interested. That is a gift I give myself. I also listen with interest as others speak. It is a gift I give to them. I take note of my surroundings with interest. It is amazing how my choice to be interested expands my awareness. I feel more alive. I throw open the shutters and regularly take deep breaths of oxygen-laden air. I know that without oxygen, my life would eventually cease to exist. I also regularly throw open the shutters of interest. I know that without cultivating a sense of interest, I only survive in life rather than thrive. A sense of curiosity adds color to my life.

Interest—Day Five

Open my eyes that I may see. Psalm 119:6

I see the interest exhibited by others and my curiosity is piqued. I willingly look at what others have discovered. I weigh their perceptions against my own. Our mutual interest sharpens our awareness like iron against iron. My curiosity is being revived. I have a healthy interest in myself, in others, and in my surroundings. This sense of deliberate attention extends to all areas of my life. Today I am discovering some wonderful gems in my spiritual readings. My attention is focused steadily on applying these truths to me personally. I am interested in the *here* as well as the *hereafter;* knowing that the *here* determines the *after*. I tuck away at least one item of interest in my mind; something new that I have learned that I would have missed with a less curious attitude. I am truly seeing life with new eyes; from a different perspective. I would have it no other way!

Interest—Day Six

Interest and curiosity, if unfettered,
spring from within like an artesian well. Axiom

I awake with the dawn and realize that a new leaf has opened before me in the book of my life. The page is uncharted and clean. I expect to succeed and to write a note of progress in my book today. My day begins to unfold. Metaphorically, I throw wide the shutters, disband all the fetters. My Higher Power wants me to succeed and is there to provide me with the wisdom and strength I need. I am living one moment at a time, one hour at a time, one day at a time. Realistic interest now thrives within me. It is part of everything I do. I am learning to pay attention and to observe. This ability enables me to cope successfully in times of sadness, disappointment, and momentary despair. The secret lies in paying attention.

Interest—Day Seven

Let the wise listen and add to their learning. Proverbs 1:5

No one can force me to take this journey; no one can stop me from taking it. I alone am responsible for the presence or absence of interest in my life. Today I take complete responsibility for interest (paying attention). This ability resides within me. I exercise it daily, as if it were a muscle. I course-correct it whenever necessary. I lean on it in difficult situations. I carry it with me, invisible yet productive; invincible yet manageable. I pay attention to the self-talk tapes about interest that play inside my head, evaluating each phrase. When I recognize a negative phrase that reinforces boredom and inattention, I make a decision to change it. I rehearse thoughts and words that help me to choose to pay attention, to remain interested in life and thriving. It is a choice and a learned skill.

Interest—Day Eight

Nothing is interesting if you're not interested. Helen MacInness

I am exploring my gifts and talents with interest, continuing to take a studious look at who I am. Today I am making a list of things I can do to make the most of who I am (e.g., taking a class, changing my hairstyle, learning a new skill, sorting my wardrobe, writing a letter). Because I'm learning to live fully, I can share with others from a vibrant, overflowing cup. I'm <u>paying attention</u> to the way my body feels as I am developing, recognizing, and honoring my personal identity versus the feelings that occur when I am denying my personal identity by overcomplying or overconforming to unrealistic or unhealthy expectations. I am unequivocally interested in all the cues my body gives me. I thoroughly relish this journey. No one ever told me that it could be this much fun!

Identify one specific behavior, in relation to interest, that you have targeted for improvement.

_____

_____

_____

_____

_____

_____

_____

Interest—Day Nine

List three points about yourself in relation to interest.

- _____

_____

- _____

_____

- _____

_____

Interest—Day Ten

You are honing the power of attention. Write down your personal affirmation related to interest.

_____

_____

_____

_____

_____

_____

_____

_____

RISKING

CHAPTER SIXTEEN
ENDORSING RISKING

Risking—Day One

Synonyms: Venturing, experimenting, speculating

Antonym: Swithering

The power to be willing to *try* is vitally important if we are to develop into assertive, confident individuals. The ability to risk is different from taking a *chance.* For example, people who purchase lottery tickets or play Russian Roulette are taking a chance. Risking means that we have evaluated the situation, have counted the cost, believe we possess the likelihood to succeed—and are willing to move forward.

If we failed to learn to risk, as adults we may agonize over the smallest decisions; become caught in the traps of worry and anxiety; be immobilized by fear. We may be unwilling to attempt the tiniest deviation from learned routines or from the script that was written for us in our family-of-origin; unable to internalize that courage is simply fear that has said its prayers.

An unknown author penned these powerful lines:

To laugh is to risk appearing the fool.
To weep is to risk appearing sentimental.
To reach out for another is to risk involvement.
To expose feelings is to risk exposing your true self.
To place your ideas and your dreams before the
crowd is to risk their loss.
To love is to risk not being loved in return.
To live is to risk dying.
To hope is to risk despair.
To try is to risk failure.
But this risk must be taken because the greatest
hazard in life is to risk nothing.
The person who risks nothing does nothing,
has nothing, and is nothing.

One may avoid suffering and sorrow, but then
simply cannot learn, feel, change, love, or grow.
Chained by certitudes, one is a slave
and has forfeited freedom.
Only a person who risks is free.

As evening was settling in and the snow was crusting over, Rich decided to try one last run down the hill. He failed to compensate for the change in the surface, took a dreadful tumble, and ended up with a broken leg. While lying there waiting for the ski patrol, he mentally reviewed his decision to try this last run. Another time, he decided, he would evaluate his fatigue level, the snow conditions, and visibility more carefully. Rich had taken a chance; not a carefully calculated risk.

We can begin learning to *risk* appropriately by deciding to move forward in life and to take action—and to like ourselves even when we make mistakes, knowing that we may learn more from our mistakes than we ever do from our successes. There is a risk in almost anything we do. That is simply the way life is.

We can look at others in a new light as well. We can learn to have confidence in them at their stage of personal growth; encouraging them to take action; supporting their efforts *to try;* allowing them the same freedom—to make mistakes and to learn precious lessons—that we allow ourselves. We know that each new day is a new beginning, the first day of the rest of our lives. We can try again and again if necessary. We can find comfort in the experience of Thomas Alva Edison. When speaking about his attempts to develop the electric light bulb, this famous inventor reportedly said, "I have not failed 10,000 times. I have successfully found 10,000 ways that will not work." Millions of people the world over benefit from his invention and are grateful that he risked trying yet again. What an example of perseverance!

Many of us learned the following words in childhood:

If at first you don't succeed; try, try again.

Sometimes we forget that this adage is as valuable in adulthood as it was during childhood.

Risking—Day Two

Table Sixteen—Problems with risking   Females—219 Males—102

	Never	Rarely	Sometimes	Frequently	Always
Females	11.0%	32.0%	36.5%	16.0%	4.5%
Males	15.7%	29.4%	34.3%	15.7%	4.9%
Overall	12.5%	31.1%	35.8%	15.9%	4.7%
Me					

Take a few moments to evaluate yourself:

- Am I usually willing to consider new ideas with a minimum of anxiety?
- Do I clearly understand the difference between taking a calculated risk and taking a chance?
- Do I experience great anxiety whenever I begin new endeavors?
- Are there problems in my life related to risking?

Risking—Day Three

We get our bread at the risk of our lives. Lamentations 5:9

I am making a list of the events in my life that have contributed to my ability to take a risk, to try. Likewise I am listing the factors that influenced me to avoid all risk or, at times, to risk unwisely. I am looking at these events and factors from a new perspective and I am learning from them. I plan to cultivate the positive and systematically eradicate the negative. I am learning to take the risks needed to live life to its fullest. There is some risk inherent in everything we do. Just as the disk jockey commented, "Getting out of bed in the morning is a risk." Today I am willing to try! I am grounded firmly in my self-worth. I know who I am. With this solid foundation, I do not fear necessary risk.

Risking—Day Four

The more I study, the more I find,
Success favors the risk-taking mind. Cherney

Timidity is no longer such a large part of my life. I am learning who I am and I am learning to take healthy risks. I realize that I can never appropriately risk too much. In the same way I am learning to have confidence in myself and my ability to try. It is exciting and I smile with delight. I accept this sense of confidence and see it reflected everywhere. I am learning to *be still* and to listen to my inner thoughts. This helps me to sort out the jumble that at times has characterized my thinking patterns. Even when my outer world is chaotic, my inner world is calm and clear. I am defining why I will risk, as well as delineating the type of evidence that will encourage me to try. Above all, I purpose to be willing to try, and try, and try yet again if that's what it takes to achieve my goals.

Risking—Day Five

Do you think anyone is going to be able to drive a wedge between
us and God's love for us? There is no way! Romans 8:36-9 (TM)

Risk spreads to all areas of life. My spiritual realm is not exempt. Risk is the price I pay for the privilege of loving. There are no guarantees of unconditional love from others; the possibility of rejection always exists. Today, however, I know that nothing separates me from God's unconditional love. That knowledge empowers me to approach others with love, unafraid of potential rejection. I choose to go after what I want, knowing I may not achieve all that I had hoped for but experiencing satisfaction because: I tried, I didn't collapse, and I learned a valuable lesson. With this information in hand, I stand prepared to try again.

Risking—Day Six

What you sow does not come to life
unless it dies. I Corinthians. 15:36

A farmer risks planting wheat (that could have been eaten) knowing that it must die to make a plentiful harvest. A thirsty traveler primes the pump with the only available container of water (water that could have been sipped) in order to receive an abundance. In a similar way, I too, am willing to risk. I am willing to invest my time and talents in order to reap a bountiful harvest. The pattern has been set before me. It has worked successfully for others; it can work for me as well. Some opportunities come only once. I step out in faith when opportunities present themselves, knowing that, while there is no guarantee that each attempt will be successful, not having tried at all guarantees failure. I am burying my old dysfunctional patterns of thinking—and am coming *alive!*

Risking—Day Seven

And the trouble is, if you don't risk
anything, you risk even more. Erica Jong

I am willing to be the person I was intended to be and to role-model confidently. I enjoy who I am and I act accordingly. I give myself full permission to succeed. Whenever I hear negative messages inside my head I simply turn the volume down. I am recording new positive messages for myself and I turn the volume up on those messages. I am creating conditions that allow me to be successful, that permit me to blossom, that encourage me in the effective use of my willpower. My cup overflows. Today I am learning more about the power of faith. I am using this knowledge to let go of the familiar and to build a bridge to my dreams. I discover options I had totally missed before and rise high above hurdles that, in the past, would have seemed insurmountable. I gain confidence in my ability to take healthy risks.

Risking—Day Eight

*Avoiding danger is no safer in the long run than
exposure. The fearful are caught as often as the bold. Helen Keller*

I am learning the difference between taking a risk and taking a chance. I no longer acquiesce to the dares of others. I have given up trying to be who others expect me to be. The price tag was too steep in terms of depression, physical illness, restlessness, unhappiness, and compulsive behaviors. Today I choose the path to health, serenity, and recovery. I have the energy and the incentive to risk carrying my goals through to completion. Awareness is everything! I keep my internal radar finely tuned. I do not seek out danger but I no longer shrink from healthy confrontation.

Identify one specific behavior, in relation to risking, that you are attempting to improve.

_____

_____

Risking—Day Nine

List three points you have learned about yourself in relation to risking.

- _____

_____

- _____

_____

- _____

_____

Risking—Day Ten

There is nothing like developing the power to be willing to try. Write your personal affirmation related to risking.

PATIENCE

CHAPTER SEVENTEEN
PERPETUATING PATIENCE

Patience—Day One

Synonyms: Composure, endurance, equanimity, fortitude

Antonym: Impatience

The power of *enduring* is a developmental task ideally honed through the twelfth and thirteenth years. If we have developed patience we possess the ability to calmly tolerate delay, to endure trouble, to persevere. The acquired skill of patience helps us to handle some ambivalence; to engage in two pursuits simultaneously (e.g., a career and a personal relationship). We can learn to produce without giving up, to be involved with several projects at one time, to be interdependent.

If we failed to develop patience, as adults we are at risk for losing self-control, for becoming easily angered or insulted. We may be unable to tolerate fatigue, thirst, temporary setbacks, and a host of other irritations that comprise the vagaries of life. We may lack the persistence, the *sticktoitiveness* that is required to accomplish and to succeed.

We have already mentioned the story of Edison. Indeed, patience is exemplified every time we turn on a light swich. It was Comte De Buffon who believed that patience really is the hallmark of genius. He described it this way,"Genius is only a greater aptitude for patience."

We often see impatience exhibited at half-time in a football game, while waiting for water to boil, or when hoping for a return phone call. Kate has found a way to contentedly wait through these unavoidable irritations. She carries a writing tablet with her at all times and writes notes to friends and family. Sometimes she finds herself hoping the phone won't ring just yet or that Billy's hair cut will take just a little bit longer, so she can address and stamp the envelope for her finished correspondence. For Kate, filling her waiting time with this activity helps to drive impatience away.

Patience requires personal discipline (as does the completion of all developmental tasks); a discipline that enables us to endure. During a seminar break, Jed and Lilly were both lamenting the time and the discipline that developing patience was requiring. "I want it to happen now," said Jed.

"I know what you mean," Lilly responded. "Since I got the picture of a better way to live, I want all my new habits in place yesterday!"

The next session began with the seminar leader saying, "As a general rule, human beings are impatient about developing patience." Jed and Lilly smiled at each other across the aisle. "It can be helpful to remember this rule of thumb", the leader continued: "Plan to spend a month of diligent recovery effort for every year of time that you spent exhibiting the less-than-desirable behavior." She did indeed give them priceless advice!

This same principle applies to whatever developmental task we are trying to complete, to whatever new habits we are working to establish. We need to understand that just as we didn't get to this point in life in a moment, neither will we arrive at instant recovery in a moment. Recovery is a process and it takes time. Developing patience is invaluable in enabling us to enjoy the process and to avoid fretting because recovery is not like instant mashed potatoes. Thank heavens! The real thing is much better—potatoes as well as solid recovery.

We can develop patience by building upon earlier developmental tasks. As the Apostle Peter wrote, we can add to our faith goodness, knowledge, self-control, and perseverance (2 Peter 1.5-8). Patience is a mind-set. The farther along we are on our reparenting journey, the healthier we are becoming in our personal and spiritual growth, the easier it will be for us to be patient. We will, after all, be able to look back at our reparenting *track-record*. This retrospection will help us to see the big picture and how patience, the ability to endure, fits into it.

In order to genuinely enjoy living and to realize our potential, we must cultivate patience. Patience allows us to tolerate and to even enjoy the questions in life—in and of themselves, apart from any answers. According to Ben Franklin, "He that can have patience can have what he will."

Patience—Day Two

Table Seventeen—Problems with patience   Females—218 Males—102

	Never	Rarely	Sometimes	Frequently	Always
Females	8.3%	35.8%	39.4%	14.2%	2.3%
Males	4.9%	27.5%	43.1%	19.6%	4.9%
Overall	7.2%	33.1%	40.6%	16.0%	3.1%
Me					

Take a few moments to evaluate yourself:

- Do I usually persevere and endure even in the face of trouble and delay?
- Am I known as an impatient person?
- Do I exhibit patience in some situations but not in others?
- What type of role-modeling did I observe in childhood?
- Do I regularly experience problems related to patience?

Patience—Day Three

Imitate those, who through faith and patience,
inherit what has been promised. Hebrews 6:12

I am making a list of the events in my life that have contributed to my developing patience, the ability to endure. Likewise I am listing the factors that influenced me to develop a lack of patience. I am looking at these events and factors from a new perspective and I am learning from them. I am expanding my list of positives and am implementing them into my life. I know that things worthwhile can never be learned without planned effort. Through consistent practice, I exhibit a willingness to learn step by step, to attain my goals slowly but surely. I practice patience and know that the ability to endure is becoming part of my character. Yes, I realize it will take more than two easy lessons and that is just fine. I keep the promise in mind.

Patience—Day Four

The really important things in life cannot be hurried. We can fly around the world in just a few hours and drive across the continent in just a few days but it still takes about nine months to make a baby—and even longer to grow oneself up. Anonymous

This journey of discovering who I am and who I was meant to be will take a lifetime. I search and study with the intent of bringing good into my life and discarding the unacceptable, dysfunctional, and inconsequential. Today I look at my choices. I choose the best, filling my life with substance. I lack nothing. I am mature and complete at this stage of my journey. Tomorrow I will advance to a higher level of maturity. I am well suited to the task at hand—that of being me and of becoming all that I can become. I realize that my timetable is not always God's timetable. I look back at frustrating events in my life and can identify reasons for delays. But in the present, I am enjoying the confidence of patient endurance. I can see my plans coming to fruition. I am contented.

Patience—Day Five

I am my own keeper. Old adage

I am learning to meet many of my own needs. I do not wait for someone else to *bring me flowers.* I am planting my own garden, growing my own blossoms, sharing them with others. My ability to be patient is extending outward to others. Along with the ancient philospher, Epictetus, I am learning to be content. Today I am giving others more room to develop according to their choosing and to progress at their own speed. I am freeing them from my expectations in this regard. I observe the way in which others exhibit patience, imitating that quality. I choose to wear a crown of contentment and patience polished by unrelenting practice and longtime exposure to the elements of life. It has weathered well. I share this gift with others. All is as it should be at this stage of my journey.

Patience—Day Six

Patience is the key to paradise. Turkish Proverb

Learning to endure helps me to be less frantic about my daily schedule. I am learning what the phrase *everything in its own time* means. I have watched children wishing to grow up quickly and I have seen elders lamenting that they seem to be hurrying toward old age much too quickly. Like Emerson, I want to adopt the pace of nature; her secret is patience. I choose to moderate the rat race but I do not confuse immobility with patience. I resist timidity but do not confuse frantic action with productive activity. Today I choose to invest the time and energy necessary to become all that I was intended to be. There is a season for everything. This is my season for growing.

Patience—Day Seven

*...being strengthened with all power...so that you
have great endurance and patience. Colossians 1:11*

My developing patience helps me to stick with my journey, to follow my path. While I do not seek conflict for its own sake, I recognize that some conflict is inherent with conquest—and I am winning daily battles. Today I view the struggles of life as the necessary prelude to satisfying progress. Developing and using patience requires a change in my philosophy of life. I am content with my growth today, knowing that I will find the way again tomorrow, and the next day, and the next. I am finding humor in the process and frequently hear my laughter. I know that the ability to laugh and to see humor in the vagaries of life contributes to my success. I identify the self-talk tapes about patience that *play* inside my head. When I recognize a negative phrase that reinforces impatience, I make a decision to change it. I am rehearsing thoughts that help me to build appropriate levels of patience, messages that will be replayed continually whether or not I am consciously aware of them.

Patience—Day Eight

There is no quality of the soul more necessary
to success and happiness than patience. Ben Franklin

I understand where I have been and I willingly course-correct. Today I watch myself grow. I notice the way in which others are growing and I can emulate positive models. I know that one cannot choose to get out of a trap until one knows that one is in the trap. In the same way, there is only one way to become a butterfly—one must be willing to stop being a caterpillar. I am willing to stop being a caterpillar. That was one stage of my life and I honor the best that I could do as a caterpillar. Now I have many more options. I can grow much more quickly. I can see so much more from my new vantage point; I have a great new perspective.

Identify one specific behavior, in relation to patience, that you are striving to improve.

_____

_____

Patience—Day Nine

List three points you have learned about your level of patience.

- _____

_____

- _____

_____

- _____

_____

Patience—Day Ten

Your power to endure is keeping you centered on your chosen path. Write down your personal affirmation related to patience.

_____

_____

_____

_____

_____

_____

_____

_____

_____

_____

_____

_____

_____

_____

RESPONSIBILITY

CHAPTER EIGHTEEN
RECOMMENDING RESPONSIBILITY

Responsibility—Day One

Synonyms: Accountability, conscientiousness, dependability

Antonym: Irresponsibility

The power of *reliable accountability* is an ongoing developmental task that needs to be solidly in place by mid-teen years. Learning to be responsible allows us to reliably accept accountability for ourselves and our behaviors as well as for the tasks we need to accomplish in life. It also indicates to others that we are dependable.

If we failed to learn responsibility, as adults we may vacillate between taking too little responsibility and assuming too much responsibility. We will be handicapped in being accountable for ourselves and our own actions. We may lack reliability with ourselves as well as with others, and consequently may experience disappointment in our relationships.

Robert had been raised in a family where he did not learn reliability and accountability. As he was the only son, his mother and three sisters waited on him hand and foot. Consequently, he failed to learn the basic concepts of responsibility. He did not develop competency in areas such as washing and ironing his clothes, preparing basic meals, and performing chores around the home.

Jennifer had a similar experience. Her parents and five brothers treated her as if she were a princess—a celebrity who should not have to lift a finger to work. As adults, both Robert and Jennifer went through a few very difficult years as they struggled to learn responsibility and to develop competence in activities of daily living. How much easier adulthood would have been if their childhood experiences had been different; if they had learned responsibility!

We must learn to hold ourselves appropriately accountable; to give up habits of procrastination, blaming, and making excuses.

We also need to be exceedingly careful about the promises we make. Realistic promises and expectations make it easier for us to follow through on them successfully.

By the same token, we need to be willing to reevaluate promises that we made unrealistically or without sufficient forethought. If we find we made some unrealistic promises, we need to discuss the need for change and revision with the parties involved. Sometimes the *party* is ourselves. Once we have renegotiated a realistic promise, then we need to be accountable to follow through on our part of the deal.

Jeff knew that the deciding factor, in whether or not his parents gave him a pet of his very own, would be how well he cared for the pets belonging to his next-door neighbors while they were away on vacation. He did very well—until the captain of the sandlot baseball team asked him to stay late for the playoffs.

Arriving home hours later, Jeff belatedly remembered the pets. Honestly but cautiously, he told his parents that the baseball game had wiped all thoughts of the pets from his mind. Now it was dark and the pets were undoubtedly very hungry. Because it was late, Dad went with him as Jeff attended to the pets. Back home, they sat down and discussed the whole situation. The upshot was that Jeff learned a valuable lesson. He learned that responsibility means seeing that his duties are taken care of even though he might not be personally available. Another time he could pay his sister or someone else to help out. And by the way, when his birthday rolled around, Jeff did receive a German shepherd puppy of his own.

When cooperating with others on a project, we must accept accountability for our portion only—not for that which is outside our control. Again, at times we may have to renegotiate or revise our plans and projects to make them appropriately manageable in terms of personal responsibility. As we gain skill in this area, we will find that we make fewer and fewer unrealistic promises and, therefore, it is easier to be accountable and reliable.

As the poet said, we have to live with ourselves and so we need to be fit for ourselves to know. Developing the power of reliable accountability is a giant step in that direction.

Responsibility—Day Two

Table Eighteen—Problems with responsibility   Females—218 Males—102

	Never	Rarely	Sometimes	Frequently	Always
Females	33.5%	41.7%	13.3%	6.9%	4.6%
Males	23.5%	38.2%	18.6%	11.8%	7.9%
Overall	30.4%	40.6%	15.0%	8.4%	5.6%
Me					

Take a few moments to evaluate yourself:

- Am I usually considered to be a reliable person, one who will carry out what I have committed myself to accomplish?
- What type of role-model am I in the area of responsibility?
- Do I exhibit financial responsibility?
- Are there problems in my life related to responsibility?

Responsibility—Day Three

Well done, good and faithful servant. Matthew 25:23.

I am making a list of the events in my life that have contributed to my developing an ability to be responsible. Likewise I am listing the factors that influenced me to develop behaviors of unreliability and unaccountability. I am looking at these events and factors from a new perspective and I am learning from them. I add to the positive list and celebrate my progress by burning the negative list. I remember that I cannot do everything but I can always do something. Today I purpose to do the best I can. I can be trusted to carry my portion of life's load. I make promises carefully because what I promise, I am faithful to fulfill. I tell myself, "So far so good!"

Responsibility—Day Four

I believe that every right implies
a responsibility. John D. Rockefeller

I have the right to be me. I realize that this means I must also be responsible for myself and my behaviors. I know that to become actualized and differentiated as an individual, I need to mature: physically, mentally, emotionally, sexually, spiritually, and socially. I want to be a *whole* person, to love myself as I am. Today I look at the big picture. I examine the patterns of my behaviors in these five areas. I take responsibility for *healing* wherein I need healing and do not settle for simply putting a bandage on areas of woundedness. I do not hold back on any part of my growth. I search for wholeness and look for specific ways in which to grow. As I grow, I feel a sense of empowerment that is visible to others. My changing thoughts are creating a pattern that my subconscious uses to help move me toward accepting responsibility for myself and my behaviors.

Responsibility—Day Five

For each one should carry his own load. Galatians 6:5

I am careful to promise only what I can fulfill. Today I take responsibility for my share of life's load; I do not promise more than I can deliver. I faithfully follow through on my promises, maintaining the trust others have placed in me. Sometimes I deliver more than I have promised and recognize that is my choice. I like the Latin phrase *Esse quam videri*—to *be* rather than to *seem*. I give up trying to pretend that I am someone different than I really am. Now that I am getting to know who I am, I waste much less time and energy trying to meet the expectations of others and those of my own that were false or unrealistic. The energy, formerly spent on *game-playing* or *masquerading*, I now direct to projects in line with my goals. Today I am gentle with myself as I responsibly continue my journey. I know who I am, rejoice in that knowledge, and go about my life with freedom to be me.

Responsibility—Day Six

*Genius consists primarily of
inspiration followed by perspiration. Proverb*

The goals and dreams that I have set before me are the inspiration that helps me to stick with this journey of personal growth. I stay centered, fully realizing that the decision to be accountable may also involve perspiration. No sweat! We either *make dust* or we *eat dust*. I choose to make dust. There is always another hill to climb and I aim to climb each one successfully. The higher I go the purer the air, the more plain the path, the more satisfying the rewards. Today I dare to walk a new path. My success yesterday inspires me today. My success today will inspire me tomorrow. It is an ever-repeating pattern. Everything in its own time.

Responsibility—Day Seven

The price of greatness is responsibility. Sir Winston Churchill

Today I am not running my life on *whim.* Accountability is always available—as needed. What a freeing state of affairs! I do not feel deprived; rather, elated. The choices I am making build my character. My character is making it easier for me to develop a balanced sense of responsibility. I realize that my mind is something like a computer: I can input thoughts and record over those that sidetrack my growth. By consistently monitoring this recording/editing process I am accomplishing that which in the past I despaired of ever completing. I am no longer thwarted by negative thought patterns passed down to me from the dysfunctional elements of my generational inheritance. I am carefully listening to my internal self-talk tapes about responsibility. I am rehearsing thoughts that help me to develop appropriate responsibility.

Responsibility—Day Eight

How quickly we become slave to our whims—whenever we practice doing the least we can get by with. Anonymous

In the past I sometimes tried to *get by.* I understand that just getting by is not the path to success. This journey is hard work. When I am tempted not to give it my all, I look back to see from where I have come. I have come a long way. I choose to maintain the ground that I have won by perseverance and hard work. I like the view from up here. The picture is larger and clearer. Today I practice being the person that I am becoming. I am choosing to be responsible, not a slave to my whims. Others recognize that I am climbing. Some cheer me on my way; they are on a similar path. This is a fine journey. Difficult at times, but very rewarding.

Identify one specific behavior, in relation to responsibility, that you are working to improve.

_____

_____

Responsibility—Day Nine

List three facts you have learned about yourself and responsibility.

- _____

_____

- _____

_____

- _____

_____

Responsibility—Day Ten

Compliment yourself. You are making strides in developing the power of reliable accountability. Write down your personal affirmation related to responsibility.

_____

_____

_____

_____

_____

_____

_____

_____

_____

_____

_____

_____

_____

_____

INTIMACY

CHAPTER NINETEEN
ESTABLISHING INTIMACY

Intimacy—Day One

Synonyms: Closeness, connection, understanding

Antonym: Disconnection

The power of *connecting* is the developmental task that requires refining ideally between the fourteenth and twentieth years of age. Intimacy involves the ability "to be me and to risk letting you see me in all my authenticity." If we learned how to be appropriately intimate, we have a sense of interdependence (as compared to one of dependence or independence). We are able to connect with the self and with others at various levels of intimacy. We can belong, be faithful in our connectedness, and be committed to the well-being of the self and others. We also have the ability to develop a spiritual relationship with a Higher Power.

If we did not learn healthy patterns of intimacy during childhood we may not know ourselves. As adults we will likely fluctuate between the fear of relationship engulfment and the fear of abandonment; between isolation and enmeshment; between self-absorption and a lack of necessary self-care. Depending upon our upbringing, we may not understand what intimacy really entails. For example, if we fail to realize that sexual activity is only one form of intimacy, we may be sexually inappropriate at times, and/or we may fail to enjoy the experience of intimacy in the other areas in which it is potentially available.

Becoming intimate with ourselves means that we take time to discover who we are and learn to be *real*—with ourselves and others. Neal was afraid to begin the process of self-discovery. "What if I don't like myself?" he asked his counselor." "Why wouldn't you?" was the reply. "Hopefully you are going to have yourself for a long time. You can always learn to do some things in a new way if you find that change is needed."

Valuing ourselves and possessing healthy personal limits predispose us to be more successful in our relationships. We have an insurance policy (so to speak) that helps us to avoid victim or offender behaviors. This also involves becoming politically smart in terms of sharing information. Initially, Daren went from one extreme to the other; from sharing nothing about himself to spilling the beans with anyone and everyone about every little personal setback. Eventually, he learned to share personal information more selectively and developed a trustworthy support system of individuals who were committed to maintaining confidentiality.

Jill had thought of intimacy in terms of physical touching only. She violated her personal boundaries several times as she struggled to be intimate with others. Gradually she came to realize that intimacy was really a mind-set; that one could be intimate in a variety of ways. She became very clear about the level of intimacy she wanted to share. This gave her a great deal of freedom to develop friendships involving differing levels of intimacy and to recognize that she had the right and the responsibility to set appropriate boundaries. With some friends she shared intellectual intimacy; with others, emotional intimacy; with still others, appropriate physical touching. Jill made a decision to reserve sexual intimacy for a marriage partner.

Becoming intimate with ourselves means that we take off the masks that we have been wearing. We tell ourselves the absolute truth about who we are and about our behaviors. As we take off these masks and let others see who we are, we may find it necessary to be more selective about those with whom we want to share ourselves. Our circle of close friends may become slightly smaller but our personal relationships can become less superficial and more nurturing.

It has been said that human beings need twelve hugs a day in order to thrive; three to just survive. We can give each other hugs in person as well as share verbal hugs over the telephone or in writing.

According to one bumper sticker, hugs are practically perfect because they are: low in energy consumption, high in energy yield, payment free, inflation proof, nonfattening, free from pesticides and preservatives, nontaxable, nonpolluting, and of course—fully returnable. Such a deal!

Intimacy—Day Two

Table Nineteen—Problems with intimacy   Females—218 Males—100

	Never	Rarely	Sometimes	Frequently	Always
Females	13.7%	29.4%	35.3%	15.6%	6.0%
Males	12.0%	31.0%	29.0%	22.0%	6.0%
Overall	13.2%	29.9%	33.3%	17.6%	6.0%
Me					

Take a few moments to evaluate yourself:

- Do I understand the different types of intimacy?
- Am I appropriately selective in the intimacy I exhibit?
- Do I readily connect with others honestly and openly?
- Am I *real* or do I frequently cover up who I am through denial and masking?
- Are there problems in my life related to intimacy?

Intimacy—Day Three

*Intimacy is simply the ability to be real, to be who we are—
and to let others see us in that unpretentious authenticity. Taylor*

I am making a list of the events in my life that have contributed to my developing an ability to be intimate with myself and appropriately intimate with others. Likewise I am listing the factors that diminished my ability to be appropriately intimate or that taught me erroneous beliefs about intimacy. I am looking at these events and factors from a new perspective and I am learning from them. I retain the positive and gladly let go of the negative. I reach deeply into the core of my being to identify my deepest and truest thoughts. I am defining different types of intimacy including intellectual, emotional, physical, sexual, spiritual and social intimacy. I don't expect one person to fulfill the entire spectrum of my intimacy needs. Today I am making clear decisions about the types of behaviors I will exhibit and with whom I will be intimate.

Intimacy—Day Four

Have God thy friend who passeth all the rest.   Tussar

One of my greatest desires is to become *real*. I am learning to be wise in knowing how and when to share who I am with others. Today I am making some personal decisions about intimacy. I believe that I am cared about, cared for, and nurtured. I am giving myself this gift and also accepting it from others. I am giving up the need to be defensive; letting go of unhealthy denial. I am thinking positive ideas that invite me to succeed. Next to befriending my Higher Power, I am becoming my own best friend and am gradually developing faith in my ability to be intimate appropriately. It is a comfortable feeling. I reward myself for the progress I am making. Each step leads to another. In moments of retrospection, I recognize and celebrate the growth I am achieving.

Intimacy—Day Five

Blessed are the peacemakers.   Matthew 5:9

I am learning to better understand myself. I cannot read another's mind; others cannot read mine. In order for another person to know my needs and wants, I must be able to identify them and express them verbally. I am learning to be wise in expressing my needs to others. I am listening to their needs, as well. I turn the lamp of my eyes to the mechanical behavioral patterns of the past. I repudiate those that have not served me well and shake off the chains of past dysfunctional programming. I am beginning to understand and accept the challenges of bona fide intimacy. I am open to trying new behaviors, behaviors that will contribute to peace. Since my brain doesn't see much difference between rehearsal and actuality, I practice the behaviors I want to exhibit. This rehearsal today will enable me to exhibit them more consistently tomorrow.

Intimacy—Day Six

*God evidently does not intend us all to be rich or powerful
but He does intend us all to be friends. Ralph Waldo Emerson*

I desire to share the true me with others. I am ridding myself of offensive behaviors. Today I am communicating honestly with myself and with others. I remember the words I saw printed on a *button*, "Please be patient; God is not finished with me yet." I give myself that gift and offer it to others. I understand that in the process of learning how to be appropriately intimate, it is important to evaluate the past, to be in the present, and to plan for the future. I have faith in my ability to handle the present as well as the future. Today I know that personal growth requires continual change. I am not apprehensive because the changes I have already made have helped me to be the person I am. I nurture my courage and as I do so, it strengthens. I welcome future changes knowing that they, too, will help me to become a more complete person and thus a better friend to myself and to others.

Intimacy—Day Seven

*The wise heart will know the
proper time and procedure. Ecclesiastes 8:5*

I am unlocking the uniqueness hidden within me. That inspires others to do likewise. Today I role-model the growth I am making. I try to give advice sparingly recognizing that like rain, the more gently advice falls the less likely it is to do damage. I pay attention to my internal self-talk related to intimacy. I evaluate each phrase for its accuracy and for its potential to assist me in learning to be appropriately intimate or its potential to sabotage my efforts. When I recognize erroneous phrases, I make an immediate decision to change them. I may not be able to *erase* all of them completely but I can turn down the volume on them and I can create new positive self-talk messages. I am rehearsing thoughts that help me to develop appropriate levels of intimacy with myself and with others.

Intimacy—Day Eight

A friend is one to whom we may pour out the contents of our hearts, chaff and grain together, knowing that the gentlest of hands will sift it, keep what is worth keeping, and with a breath of kindness, blow the rest away. Arabian Definition

My aim is not to remake myself, rather simply to bring to the surface that which is within me. It is electrifying to discover who I am and to realize that entity has been there all along—albeit somewhat obscured by pretense, by the ashes of shattered dreams, by the clutter of ineffectual bandages layered over woundedness, by a frightful collage of impediments acquired along the way. In the past I was simply too busy or too preoccupied to recognize the magnitude of my intrinsic worth. Today I make a commitment to remove the debris, to heal the woundedness, and to allow the one-of-a-kind essence of my being to flourish. I don't try to mimic another whom I admire. I simply nurture my individuality. It is thriving. My authenticity shines through.

Identify one specific behavior, in relation to intimacy, that you are working to improve.

_____

_____

Friendship is so many things.
It is feeling completely natural with another,
Forgetting all pretense—and just being yourself.
It is sharing both big and little things,
Joy and sorrow, laughter and tears.
It is counting on another to understand your moods,
To put up with your failings,
To be there when needed most—
With a word of encouragement, a smile, a look...
—Unknown

Intimacy—Day Nine

Give yourself kudos. You are identifying the different types of intimacy and learning to exhibit behaviors appropriate to each. List three discoveries about yourself in relation to intimacy.

- _____

  _____

- _____

  _____

- _____

  _____

Intimacy—Day Ten

Celebrate! Congratulate yourself on the progress you are making in developing the power of *connecting.* Write down your personal affirmation related to intimacy.

_____

_____

_____

_____

_____

_____

BOUNDARIES

CHAPTER TWENTY
SHOWCASING BOUNDARIES

Boundaries—Day One

Synonyms: Borders, demarcations, limits, perimeters

Antonym: Boundaryless

The power of setting limits is a developmental task that ideally builds upon skills learned from infancy onward. The ability to create and consistently implement desirable personal limits is a prerequisite for becoming appropriately intimate with ourselves and with others. Bona fide boundaries enable us to protect ourselves, to become interdependent, to thrive in life.

If we did not build appropriate boundaries during childhood, if we were not permitted to say *no,* if our willpower was broken, if there were no role-models to teach us how to set healthy personal limits, we are at risk for experiencing boundary problems. As adults we risk becoming victims or offenders, unaware of where our personal boundaries end and those of another begin. We may vacillate between isolation and enmeshment, between boundaries that are too rigid or too lax. We will likely fail to develop productive relationships.

The task of learning to develop personal limits can be intimidating if we attempt to complete the process all at once. It is much better to take one portion at a time. Like the five-year-old who was interviewed by Art Linkletter: "Can you tell your right from your left?"

"No," the child replied.

"Well, then, what do you know?" Linkletter persisted.

"I know my front from my back."

Metaphorically, we can begin by knowing *our front from our back* and proceed to learn our right from our left. First, we need to identify our current boundaries in at least five main areas: physical, mental, emotional, sexual, and spiritual. Secondly, we need to determine whether or not our present boundaries are effective and desirable in adulthood. We need to make certain that each boundary is of our own choosing. In some cases, our boundaries may be too loose, too tight, or totally nonexistent. We need to create bona fide boundaries in each area. When one is in place, we will likely discover another that needs development or revision, and yet another, and still another. Without balanced personal boundaries, others can encroach upon our lives and our time, leaving us with little or no time for ourselves.

Because of stress-related symptoms and emotional exhaustion, June found herself sitting first in the doctor's office and later in that of a counselor. She had totally devoted her time and energy to the needs of her family, the children's school, her church, and her job. Whenever she was asked to help or to be in charge of a project, she readily volunteered. With her low sense of self-esteem, she had overcompensated by directing her energies outwardly in an effort to see herself as worthwhile. She took great pride in the fact that no one else could do the job as well, that she was truly *needed*. Unfortunately, June had not set effective personal limits and there was no time in her frantic schedule for self-care and personal growth.

With guidance and encouragement, June learned to prioritize; to more efficiently allocate her time and resources. She learned to set healthy, functional limits. As a result, she now role-models bona-fide-boundary development in her daily pursuits and is delighted to report that the world has kept turning. In fact, her personal world is turning much more successfully.

It can be more difficult to develop and consistently implement personal limits when the people with whom we spend great amounts of time do not value what we are trying to do or attempt to tear down our efforts. We may need to reevaluate our relationships, selecting family-of-choice friends from among those who understand boundary building and who are committed to personal growth.

Creating and consistently implementing bona fide boundaries is the process of a lifetime—one step builds upon another. It is hard work; very hard work. But the efforts pay appreciable dividends on a daily basis.

Boundaries—Day Two

Table Twenty—Problems with boundaries   Females—217 Males—100

	Never	Rarely	Sometimes	Frequently	Always
Females	11.1%	30.8%	33.2%	21.2%	3.7%
Males	17.0%	30.0%	31.0%	19.0%	3.0%
Overall	12.9%	30.6%	32.5%	20.5%	3.5%
Me					

Take a few moments to evaluate yourself:

- Do I usually implement and maintain appropriate personal limits regardless of the expectations or the coercion of others?
- Are my boundaries too rigid?
- Are my boundaries too loose?
- Do I have problems related to boundary mastery?

Boundaries—Day Three

When the Most High...divided all mankind,
He set up boundaries for the peoples. Deuteronomy 32:8

I am making a list of the events in my life that have contributed to my developing bona fide boundaries. Likewise I am listing the factors that influenced me to fail in developing healthy personal limits. I am looking at these events and factors from a new perspective and I am learning from them. My previous choices regarding personal limits resulted in my being who I am now; they will keep me trapped at this level if I continue them *as is.* Today I assess my boundaries and set healthier limits in one department of my choosing. I understand the discipline that is required to create and maintain this personal limit. I have the necessary discipline. The results are well worth the effort. I expand my awareness by devoting time to study. I find that our universe operates smoothly within boundaries of many types—seas and shores, suns and planets, atoms and molecules. My personal world, also, needs appropriate boundaries in order to run efficiently.

Boundaries—Day Four

*In some cases it is advantageous to build
a breakwater as well as a lighthouse. Cherney*

Balanced boundaries are now present in my life on a daily basis. I am strong in my trust and realistic in my expectations. Because I am sure of my hope, I pass it on freely to others. Today is the first day of the rest of my life—a life that now includes effective personal limits. I remind myself that even though I have not yet discovered the sum and substance of my uniqueness, I am enjoying the quest. I am certain that I will continue to discover the uniqueness that is me and purpose not to stall my journey by allowing old habit patterns to *derail* me. I also understand the philosophy of prevention—an ounce of it is worth a pound of cure! Some of my progress I see already; some I do not but I am certain it is there. I continue the building project with an emphasis on prevention.

Boundaries—Day Five

*The ability to create and consistently implement
appropriate personal limits is a gift that enriches all. Anonymous*

I am looking inside to discover the boundaries that are *right* for me. Today I am setting my personal limits with firmness and with kindness. Likewise I am learning that when someone else sets a boundary I need not take it personally. It is simply a statement of limits that I honor. I do not make a judgment about their personal limits. The rights of others are as important to them as mine are to me. When my boundaries have been violated I make a decision about placing myself in a similar position in the future. If I have invaded the boundaries of others, I know that I can learn a *new way*. I can select healthier behaviors to exhibit. I am growing in my ability to guard my boundaries and to respect the personal limits of those whose lives I touch. This gift, all too rare, enriches both them and me.

Boundaries—Day Six

Good fences make good neighbors. Robert Frost

Boundary setting often involves being able to understand the extremes of an idea. Today I am looking at the spectrum of behaviors that presently harmonize with my personal limits, realizing that a variety of behaviors can be appropriate depending upon the situation. I am not limited to only one choice. It is a joy to realize the diversity of my options. For instance, my *fences* can be composed of a plain yes or no, decorated with kind firmness, or ornate with collaborative ideas. My fences are furnished with gates that may be opened at any time. It is my choice. Life is a gift that I choose not to take for granted. I inhale deeply, savoring the treat of fresh air that is now enriching my life. I savor the power of positive expectation that now winds through my days like a thread of gold. My development of functional personal boundaries is enabling me to be a very good neighbor.

Boundaries—Day Seven

*Owning our boundaries does not mean that we
will always like our every deed, word, or thought;
it does mean we take responsibility for them. Taylor*

I am carefully listening to messages that *play* in my mind about boundary setting. I pay attention to what I hear. I evaluate my internal tapes for their potential to help me create and implement bona fide boundaries. When I recognize phrases that can slow my progress or sabotage the development of healthier personal limits, I make a decision to change them. I turn down the volume on them and concentrate instead on creating new positive self-talk messages. I rehearse thoughts that help me to develop appropriate boundaries. These messages are replayed continually whether or not I am consciously aware of them. This exercise is helping me to be successful in building bona fide boundaries.

Boundaries—Day Eight

You either control your
boundaries or they control you. Old Adage

I am defining exactly what I expect to accomplish and believe I am successful. I have *let go* of some of the excess baggage I have carried around for years. I feel calm and energized, excited and accepting. It feels great and empowering to have unfettered my life so that I can make a positive contribution to myself and to others. Today I am paying attention to the way my body feels. I am learning to recognize more quickly the sensations that accompany boundary violations. I am alert to the cues my body gives me and use the information to help me make decisions that are beneficial both now and in the long term. My, how I enjoy this journey!

Identify one behavior, in relation to boundary mastery, on which you are specifically working.

_____

Boundaries—Day Nine

List three things you have learned about yourself in relation to boundary mastery.

- _____

_____

- _____

_____

- _____

_____

Boundaries—Day Ten

Learning to create and consistently implement balanced personal limits is an ongoing process. Write down your personal affirmation related to boundary mastery.

_____

_____

_____

_____

_____

_____

_____

_____

_____

_____

_____

_____

_____

_____

_____

INTEGRITY

CHAPTER TWENTY-ONE
PRIORITIZING INTEGRITY

Integrity—Day One

Synonyms: Incorruptibility, goodness, honesty, uprightness

Antonym: Dishonesty

The power of *virtue* is an ongoing developmental task that involves establishing a predisposition and commitment to honesty, purity, and uprightness. If we developed integrity, we learned rectitude versus corruptibility in the midst of a culture wherein almost anything and anyone can be bought if the price is right.

If we did not develop integrity, as adults we are at risk for living dishonest lives be that in the area of standards, morals, career, personal relationships, or spirituality. In fact, we may find it difficult if not impossible to distinguish between right and wrong, between truth and error; between who we are and who others think we are or expect us to be.

One day, Johnny came home from school and asked his mother for a definition of integrity. She replied, "I've always liked your father's definition. He says that a person with integrity is someone with whom you could play chess over the phone."

"But I don't play chess," the boy answered coyly.

"I know," said his mother, "but you do play marbles for keeps."

"Okay, I get it," Johnny replied. "Thanks for giving me an idea for my presentation in class tomorrow."

As we develop habits of honesty and virtue, we must learn to accept the initial discomfort that comes from telling ourselves the absolute, microscopic truth—especially if our previous habit patterns involved denial, pretending, minimization, and mislabeling. We need to realize that a little white lie is still an untruth and will only serve to delay our personal growth. When we are tempted to overexplain, to embellish the facts, to slant information in our favor, to color explanations in a attempt to vindicate or defend ourselves, to assuage painful feelings, or to caretake—the old adage *silence is golden* can be a potent remedy.

We can begin developing integrity by making a commitment to be completely honest—with ourselves first and then with others. We can identify, analyze, and understand that old behaviors of prevarication (that we may have developed during childhood in an effort to protect ourselves from some perceived danger) are no longer of any real benefit to us in adulthood.

We also need to identify and analyze the role-modeling we received in the arena of integrity. If we lacked appropriate role-models during childhood, it is never too late to select a role-model in adulthood who exhibits the type of integrity we desire to develop. In addition, we can study about historical figures who exhibited honest, upright behaviors. For example, go to the library and check out a book on Abraham Lincoln; a man so renowned for his integrity that he was aptly nicknamed, Honest Abe. Many stories have been written about his life; stories that reflect his basic predisposition toward honesty; anecdotes that define his upright character. This study can stimulate us to reflect on the behaviors we will choose to exhibit.

John Ruskin believed that, "To make your children capable of honesty is the beginning of education." That is a good beginning place and a desirable goal for everyone—regardless of age.

Integrity—Day Two

Table Twenty-one—problems with integrity   Females—218 Males—102

	Never	Rarely	Sometimes	Frequently	Always
Females	33.0%	46.8%	13.3%	4.1%	2.8%
Males	26.5%	38.2%	17.6%	11.8%	5.9%
Overall	30.9%	44.1%	14.6%	6.6%	3.8%
Me					

Take a few moments to evaluate yourself:

- Do I usually exhibit high standards of integrity in all my interactions?
- Do I tell <u>myself</u> the absolute truth on a consistent basis?

- Do I lack the ability to maintain virtuous interactions with myself and others?
- Are there problems in my life related to integrity?

Integrity—Day Three

The integrity of the upright guides them. Proverbs 11:3

I am making a list of the events in my life that have contributed to my developing integrity. Likewise I am listing the factors that influenced me to develop an inadequate supply of virtue. I am looking at these events and factors from a new perspective and I am learning from them. I am keeping the lists handy for ready reference to remind me of the direction in which I am heading. Today I am developing behaviors that reflect integrity. I possess the wealth of honesty. It embellishes my character like fine gold decorates the altar of my favorite cathedral. It guides my daily activities. Each person I meet recognizes my standards. My true friends rejoice in my presence and honor my choices. I tell the truth because it is part and parcel of my authenticity.

Integrity—Day Four

There is nothing so powerful as truth. Daniel Webster

When all is said and done, I must live with who I am and the choices I have made. I am choosing to develop integrity. It forms a framework for my thoughts, feelings, and behaviors. I am accepted by me and by those I encounter. Today I live each moment truthfully. I am honest with myself and with each person with whom I deal. I am accepted for who I am and for what I do today. What I have not yet achieved is not an issue because I am still in process. *Sincere, consistent, reliable,* and *real* are words that describe me. I am taking care of myself. I sleep well, knowing that I have honestly not shirked my responsibility. I do not wait for others to act; I do not push them to act. I take action for myself— now.

Integrity—Day Five

*Have you considered my servant Job? There is no
one on earth like him...he still maintains his integrity. Job 2:3*

I am developing a reputation for truth and integrity. I enjoy knowing that there is one less rascal in this world. Even when it would be more comfortable to *tell a little white lie,* I am learning to *live* the truth. I study the life of Job and purpose to maintain my integrity. I know that I am headed in the right direction. Today I take another step toward developing the habit of integrity. Each small step moves me closer to that goal. Others feel at ease knowing they are dealing with a person of integrity. The power of virtue surrounds me at all times. Peace goes before me; peace follows.

Integrity—Day Six

*Character is like a tree and reputation is like its shadow.
The shadow is what we think of it; the tree is the real thing.
Abraham Lincoln*

I have every right to be alive; to be happy and joyful. I gladly envision the person I was intended to be, the individual I am choosing to become. The process is never finished and is not the same for anyone else. Today I am just where my Higher Power intends me to be—receptive to learning. I cherish my own uniqueness; I respect that of others. I am no longer embarrassed by mistakes; they are stepping-stones to new choices—discreet choices. Many times in the past I have weathered embarrassment on behalf of others. I now choose not to be embarrassed by the actions of others. I am giving up the need to try to control the behaviors of others through embarrassment. I enjoy being free of that excess baggage. I am choosing to be the real thing.

Integrity—Day Seven

*...we know how troubles can develop passionate patience in us,
and how that patience, in turn, forges the tempered steel of virtue.
Romans 5:3 (TM)*

I am carefully listening to my self-talk messages about integrity. I pay attention to what I hear, evaluating each phrase for its potential to assist me in learning to exhibit integrity or its potential to diminish that ability. When I recognize a negative phrase, I make a decision to change it. I turn down the volume on those old negative words and concentrate instead on creating new positive self-talk messages. I am rehearsing thoughts that help me to integrate appropriate principles into my lifestyle. These internal messages are replayed continually whether or not I am consciously aware of them. This exercise is helping me to develop and to exhibit integrity on a consistent basis.

Integrity—Day Eight

*If you tell the truth, you don't
have to remember anything. Mark Twain*

Honesty burns within me like a glowing ember. It contributes to my happiness. I do not run after it as if chasing a shadow. The power of integrity gives me the courage to approach others for help in making my dreams come true. I do not fear asking for help to achieve the results I dream of. With the aid of my Higher Power and trusted friends, I see my dreams being fulfilled. Today I am not disappointed in myself or in the progress I am making. I am gently encouraging myself to be consistent in expecting success while at the same time refusing to be harsh with myself when I make mistakes. A mistake simply gives me a clue about ways in which I can make different choices another time. It is amazing how my memory seems to be improving!

Identify one specific behavior, in relation to integrity, that you are working to improve.

_____

_____

_____

_____

Integrity—Day Nine

Reward yourself for the progress you are making in developing the power of *virtue*. List three particulars you have learned about yourself in your study of integrity.

• _____

_____

• _____

_____

• _____

_____

Integrity—Day Ten.

Good work! Compliment yourself on your progress. Write down your personal affirmation related to integrity.

CREATIVITY

CHAPTER TWENTY-TWO
HEADLINING CREATIVITY

Creativity—Day One

Synonyms: Artistry, giftedness, ingenuity, inventiveness

Antonym: Nongenerativity

The power to *generate* is a developmental task that is also ongoing. Creativity enables us to use our innate gifts to make a positive contribution in life; to individually accept responsibility for making this world a better place in which to live. It enables us to act in a productively inventive manner.

If we did not learn creativity, as adults we may be satisfied with taking; with being sponges or parasites instead of pulling our own weight. We may have no concept of our responsibility to contribute to the betterment of our world—simply because we live in it. We may suffer from stagnation and wallow in the pit of immature egocentricity.

The Bible tells us that we need to become as little children. Why? Perhaps because they can be so creative. You may recall hearing the story about the little girl who prayed a very unusual bedtime prayer. "Dear God," the child began, then carefully recited all the letters of the alphabet and ended with "Amen." A bit puzzled, her mother asked about the unusual prayer.

"I didn't know what to say to God tonight," the daughter replied. "But God will know how to put the letters together into the right words for me."

Stan and Laura regularly brainstorm with their children during an activity they call "create a secret surprise." The whole family participates. Each week they create a secret surprise for someone else. In the past they have paid the bridge toll for the car behind them, purchased groceries and placed them on the porch of a needy family, raked the lawn for a neighbor who was at the doctor's office and sent community concert tickets to a lonely widow.

At first, it was difficult to come up with ideas. As time went by, however, it became easier and easier. Now, not only do they have fun, the children are learning the rewards of creativity, as well. Most of the time they actually brainstorm more ideas than they can implement!

We can stimulate our creativity by first deciding that our efforts do not have to be spectacular. We must decide that we are willing to be our unique selves. We can become comfortable expressing ourselves in a way that *works* for us even though our style may differ from that of others.

We can consciously look for ways in which to make creative contributions to our own lives and to the lives of others—contributions beyond those involved with our chosen career. The contributions do not have to be extravagant; they can be as spontaneous and unrehearsed as a smile bestowed upon a weary traveler. We contribute based on our innate talents. We do not contribute to receive gratitude or remuneration but because we genuinely want to make this world a better place in which to live.

Creativity—Day Two

Table Twenty-two—Problems with creativity   Females—216 Males—102

	Never	Rarely	Sometimes	Frequently	Always
Females	24.5%	35.2%	26.9%	10.6%	2.8%
Males	27.4%	37.3%	18.6%	11.8%	4.9%
Overall	25.5.%	35.8%	24.2%	11.0%	3.5%
Me					

Take a few moments to evaluate yourself:

- Do I readily generate new ideas and ways in which to accomplish my goals?
- Do I find myself stuck in a rut most of the time?
- Am I usually stumped or immobile when circumstances suddenly change and a different response is required?
- Am I excited or frightened by the possibility of generating new ideas?
- Do I experience problems related to creativity?

Creativity—Day Three

Where there is no vision the people perish. Proverbs 29:18

I am making a list of the events in my life that have contributed to my developing an ability to use my creativity. Likewise I am listing the factors that influenced me to deny my innate creativity or to fail in developing it. I am looking at these events and factors from a new perspective and I am learning from them. The school of inventive genius is one from which I never plan to graduate. Today I look for one opportunity to use my creativity. I enjoy varying some of the *routines* that have become mundane. Within my sphere of influence, I generate ideas that help to improve my quality of life and that of those around me. These visionary ideas, however simple, help me to thrive.

Creativity—Day Four

Bite off more than you can chew.
Then chew it.
Plan for more than you can do.
Then do it.
Hitch your wagon to a star.
Keep your seat—and there you are.
Unknown

Today I am clearly seeing who I am becoming. I ask for clear vision so (in the words of Peter Marshall) I may know where to stand and what to stand for. I realize that I unless I stand for something I shall fall for anything. Silence is a great starting place for creativity. There is a vast silence in the universe. Mentally I connect myself to a star and my creativity blossoms as it basks in the illuminating silence of the ages. As I leave the noise of the world behind I glimpse the big picture and my place in it. I know that the ancestor of every action is a thought, even though sometimes that thought is not within my conscious awareness. I keep my wagon hitched to the star of creativity. This is an amazing journey!

Creativity—Day Five

Our most valuable contribution
to the world is ourselves. Anonymous

Everyone has something to learn and everyone has something to share. No one can share exactly what I can share because no one else is exactly like me. Therefore, I can give the world a gift that no one else can give. Being myself and sharing who I am with others is a unique contribution. It is exciting to identify my creative contribution day by day, moment by moment, knowing that it is valuable and *one of a kind.* My contribution never diminishes; rather it enhances who I am. I spend little time in thinking about *if only* or *what if.* My time has arrived and I am ready. Today I am the hero of my own story, the philanthropist of my own valuable contribution to this world.

Creativity—Day Six

What lies behind us and what lies before us are tiny
matters—compared to what lies within us. Oliver Wendell Holmes

I am thankful for who I am, exactly as I am. I am turning my mistakes into stepping-stones that lead me steadily upward. I am discovering who I am and I like who I am. My heart is strengthened by hopes fulfilled. I lay hold of my dreams with tenacity knowing that positive expectations are birthed within me. Today my life flows more smoothly because creativity sings in my heart. I step forward confidently, knowing that I can cope with whatever needs to be managed and accomplished in my life. I am glad that there is no such a thing as bad weather; there are only different types of weather. I expect some rough seas. I expect to learn from the past, the present, and the future as I assertively embrace life. Fortune favors the bold. It is so exhilarating to be boldly creative!

Creativity—Day Seven

If your mind can conceive it you can achieve it. Anonymous

Today I am carefully listening to my self-talk messages about creativity. I pay attention to what I hear, evaluating each phrase for its accuracy and for its potential to allow my creativity to flourish or for its potential to stifle. When I recognize negative messages, I make a decision to change them. I may not be able to *erase* all of them completely but I can turn down the volume on them. I create new positive self-talk messages. I am rehearsing thoughts that help me to enhance my creativity. These messages are replayed continually whether or not I am consciously aware of them. This exercise is helping me to successfully mine the creativity that lives within me. It is so much fun!.

Creativity—Day Eight

*Champions of creativity are often
commissioned by the vicissitudes of life. Lawrence*

I rejoice to realize that creativity lives within me, steadily matching every heartbeat. It has been said that necessity is the mother of invention. However, I choose to be creative without any external motivators. The power to generate, to make a positive contribution, is a gift I give myself, a gift I pass along to others. I see myself becoming complete, mature, confident, productive, and gratefully joyful. Creativity enfolds me with serenity. Strain and pressure do not invade my internal world. When it is present, adversity seems to motivate my best efforts at ingenious inventiveness. If I experience a moment of doubt, positive expectations rise from a deep wellspring within me and bubble up. Today I smile as I turn to that artesian spring of expectation within and savor the ever-present refreshment available to me. Life is good.

Identify one specific behavior, in relation to creativity, that you are determined to improve.

_____

_____

_____

_____

_____

_____

Creativity—Day Nine

List three discoveries you have made about yourself in relation to creativity.

- _____

_____

- _____

_____

- _____

_____

Creativity—Day Ten

Be creative in acknowledging your progress. Write down your personal affirmation related to creativity.

_____

_____

_____

_____

_____

_____

_____

_____

_____

_____

_____

_____

_____

_____

_____

LOVE

CHAPTER TWENTY-THREE
CHAMPIONING LOVE

Love—Day One

Synonyms: Adoration, appreciation, regard

Antonyms: Hate, indifference

The power of *affection* and *devotion* is potentially enhanced as we appropriately complete the developmental tasks of childhood. We learn to love ourselves and others; we learn to love our Higher Power—to tap into that source of energy and regeneration. Love involves acknowledging individual freedom of choice and encouraging the self and others to become all that they were intended to be.

If we did not learn to love, as adults we may be at risk for becoming dependent on or addicted to, someone or something outside of ourselves in an attempt to feel good about ourselves. We will risk caretaking instead of caring. *Caring* involves healthy nurturing of the self as well as others with a goal of supporting everyone to become as actualized and differentiated as possible. Caring shares from an overflowing cup.

Caretaking involves doing for others what they are capable of doing for themselves. It gives from a well of unmet needs, usually in an attempt to boost the caretaker's own feelings of value. It causes fatigue, resentment, and personal burnout; it deprives others of the chance to take responsibility for personal growth. Caretaking does not help anyone because an empty cup has nothing of value to share.

Society has so romanticized and sentimentalized the concept of love that it is greatly misunderstood. What is love, really? There have been endless attempts to explain it. The dictionary devotes more than half a column to defining love, using words such as devotion, affection, attachment, or God's benevolent concern for humankind.

Most of us have heard statements such as, "Love is a principle, not a feeling." That can be confusing to some because strong emotions and feelings are often connected with love. In and of itself, love is neither an emotion nor a feeling; it is a skill, a choice that involves our thoughts, our mind-set, our behaviors, our verbal and nonverbal communication. It can trigger the rise of a whole range of emotions and feelings.

Someone has said:

A bell is just a bell, until you ring it;
A song is just a song, until you sing it;
A day is just a day, until you live it;
A candle is just a candle, until you light it;
And love is only love—until you give it!

As with almost everything in life, it is virtually impossible to share effectively that which we do not know ourselves. If we were not taught how to love appropriately, we need to teach ourselves that skill now. Some individuals find it helpful to internalize the concept that their Higher Power represents love. Through this metaphor they experience love personally, often for the first time. We can also learn something of love from the experience of others. We can read stories about individuals who learned how to love versus those who *blew it.* We can be willing to give love—to ourselves first, and then to others.

It is important to recognize that offering love unconditionally to ourselves and to others takes time and effort. It comes in different packages and is displayed in different ways. What works for one may not work for another, but we can all do something. Some choose to travel halfway around the world to help with disaster relief; others assist in good-Samaritan shelters and food kitchens; some write notes or make phone calls to the homebound; still others take their pets to visit residents of rest homes. Remember that some benefit accrues to the one who risks *loving*, whether or not that love is reciprocated.

While sorting through boxes after her mother died, Dolores found an old scrapbook filled with clippings, poems, and short prose. Each had been pasted into the book with care. Each obviously had held special meaning for her mother. Dolores shared the following verses with us. Written by an unknown author, they challenge us to scatter loving words.

Loving words will cost but little,
Journeying up the hill of life;
But they make the weak and weary
Stronger, braver, for the strife.
Do you count them only trifles?
What to earth are sun and rain?
Never was a kind word wasted,
Never one was said in vain.

When the cares of life are many,
And its burdens heavy grow,
Think of weak ones close beside you—
If you love them, tell them so.
What you count of little value
Has an almost magic power,
And beneath their cheering sunshine
Hearts will blossom like a flower.

So, as up life's hill we journey,
Let us scatter all the way
Kindly words, for they are sunshine
In the dark and cloudy day.
Grudge no loving word or action
As along through life you go,
There are weary ones around you—
If you love them, tell them so.

Sometimes we ourselves are the weary ones. Regardless of the way in which love is shown, it starts at home. We need to learn to genuinely love ourselves; to look in the mirror and say, "I love you"—and mean it! We need to use our creativity to nurture ourselves and then use it again to discover ways in which we can lovingly share our overflowing cup with others. The rewards are boundless and recompense our efforts many times over.

Love—Day Two

Table Twenty-three—Problems with love   Females—218 Males—102

	Never	Rarely	Sometimes	Frequently	Always
Females	19.7%	35.3%	28.4%	12.0%	4.6%
Males	17.6%	29.4%	31.4%	15.7%	5.9%
Overall	19.1%	33.4%	29.4%	13.1%	5.0%
Me					

Take a few moments to evaluate yourself:

- Do I view love primarily in terms of romantic sentimentalism?
- Do I regularly exhibit unconditional love for myself and for others regardless of gender, age, race, status, culture, position, or behaviors?
- Is my ability to exhibit affection and devotion based on whim or on a carefully cultivated mind-set?
- Are there problems in my life related to my ability to love?

Love—Day Three

There is no room in love for fear. 1 John 4:18 (TM)

I am making a list of the events in my life that have contributed to my developing an ability to love myself, my Higher Power, and others. Likewise I am listing the factors that influenced me to fail to develop an ability to love or to exhibit affection appropriately. I am looking at these events and factors from a new perspective and I am learning from them. They provide the awareness that is necessary for positive growth. Sometimes I feel that I am in step with others and sometimes I feel out of step. Today I no longer fear when I feel temporarily out of sync. I understand that, although the rhythm may be different, I need to follow my internal drummer. The beat is clear and strong. It's comforting to hear the sound and to know that I am marching on the right path—and at the right tempo—for me. Sometimes my drummer matches that of others and sometimes it doesn't. Either way, it's okay.

Love—Day Four

The ultimate lesson all of us have to learn is unconditional love which includes not only others but ourselves as well.
Elizabeth Kubler-Ross

I feel genuine affection for myself. I am taking personal inventory and realize how much I have grown. This is a happy realization! Today I am practicing unconditional love. It is reflected in my actions, both to myself and to others. They are encouraged as they watch my consistent and steady progress. I share with them by being who I am and simply letting them see the person that I am becoming. I have given up the need to try to figure out the motives of others. Rather, I concentrate on my choices and try to understand my motivation. Even when my behaviors *fall short* of my goals, I still love myself. I pay attention to the way my body feels. I am learning to recognize the sensations that accompany unconditional love versus those that accompany an attempt to control the actions of others. I am choosing to work with my body in the promulgation of positive sensations. Love is so becoming!

Love—Day Five

Of all earthly music, that which reaches farthest into heaven is the beating of a truly loving heart. Henry Ward Beecher

My goal is to refrain from intentionally hurting myself or another. Today I am exhibiting sibling affection and kindness to others. I am uplifting and nurturing the persons in my life, supporting their hopes and dreams whenever possible. Their success does not diminish mine. We make different contributions; all are needed and all are valuable. I do not search for people to cheer and applaud my efforts. I applaud myself and offer that gift to others, as well. I strive to apply the golden rule from the depths of a truly loving heart. I exhibit the music of unconditional love, realizing that, at least to some degree, I am capable of separating the behavior from the person. Unconditional love is the oil that brings harmony to our lives.

Love—Day Six

Love others as well as you love yourself. Mark 12:29 (TM)

I realize that the quality of the unconditional love I offer to myself will be reflected in the love I offer to others. The lamp of my soul is alight with love; with love for myself, for others, for life, and for my Higher Power. I see everything through the eyes of love—and somehow the imperfections in and around me are less distinct and less irritating. I know that I learn to love by loving. Practice makes perfect, as the old saying goes. Today my aim is to be loving to myself and to others with no thought of return. I purpose to set aside shallow, narcissistic definitions of love and to develop a consistent mind-set; one that is not indulged on a whim or on the basis of romantic sentimentalism. My prayer is that of St. Francis of Assisi: grant that I may not so much seek to be consoled as to console; to be understood as to understand; to be loved as to love. The love that dwells within my heart will never be washed away. It is permanently installed with both a reserve and an overflow.

Love—Day Seven

And now these three remain: faith, hope, and love—
but the greatest of these is love. I Corinthians 13:13

I am carefully listening to my internal self-talk tapes about love. I pay conscious attention and evaluate each one. When I recognize an erroneous message that diminishes my belief that I am lovable or that I am capable of exhibiting unconditional love, I make a decision to change it. I *turn-down* the volume on those old, unhelpful messages and concentrate instead on recording new, positive self-talk messages. Today I am rehearsing thoughts and words that help me to love myself, my Higher Power, and others. These messages are replayed continually whether or not I am consciously aware of them. They positively contribute to my ability to love judiciously. I understand the tremendous power of genuine love. It is indeed one of the greatest gifts.

Love—Day Eight

Love is the universal key that unlocks all doors. Anonymous

Becoming who I am is a journey within a journey. I am part of the journey of life and my individual journey is to become the person I was intended to be. The process is one of continual discovery. Love is the key that unlocks doors on my journey. I know who I am and yet today I will learn something new about myself. Tomorrow, next week, next year I will still be who I am and I will have learned much more about myself; I will be more whole, more advanced, and more polished. On this fascinating journey I am my own best friend. It is comforting to know that I am always there for myself. I continually affirm my progress and do not limit my potential successes by setting limits on who I can become.

Identify one specific behavior, in relation to love, that you are seeking to enhance.

_____

_____

_____

_____

LETTING GO

Letting go doesn't mean to stop caring,
It means I can't do it for someone else.
It is to admit powerlessness,
Which means the outcome is not in my hands.

It's not cutting myself off,
It's the realization that I cannot control another.
It is not to enable—
But to allow learning from natural consequences.

It is not to try to change or blame another—
I can only change myself.
It is not to care for, but to care about;
It is not to fix, but to be supportive.

It is not to judge,
But to allow another to be a human being.
It is not to be in the middle arranging all the outcomes.
It is to allow others to effect their own outcomes.

It is not to criticize and regulate anyone,
But to try what I dream I can be.
It is not to be protective but to permit another to face reality.
It is to fear less and love more.

—Anonymous

Love—Day Nine

List three attributes you have learned about yourself in relation to
your ability to love.

- _____

_____

- _____

_____

- _____

_____

Love—Day Ten

Learning to love, especially learning to love yourself unconditionally, is a major task. Write down your personal affirmation related to love.

_____

_____

_____

_____

_____

_____

_____

_____

_____

_____

_____

_____

_____

_____

EQUIPOISE

CHAPTER TWENTY-FOUR
EXPEDITING EQUIPOISE

Equipoise—Day One

Synonyms: Equilibrium, composure, stability

Antonym: Instability

The power of maintaining *balance* is necessary if we are to avoid needless upheaval and experience relative unflappability in life. Developing balance is an ongoing learning process although the stage may be set during adolescence for an easier or more difficult course. It can take between thirty and fifty years to really get to know ourselves and to realize optimum balance most of the time. Achieving stability means that we use willpower, responsibility, creativity, and the skills of other completed developmental tasks to take action in a timely and appropriate manner.

If we did not learn equipoise during adolescence, as adults we may not know how to achieve stability. We may be unable to adjust our patterns of living or course-correct in a timely enough manner to avoid wide fluctuations. We may include even desirable activities to excess and exclude others that would benefit us.

We often think of balance in terms of acrobatics. Our language recognizes this in idioms such as *walking a straight line* and *walking a tightrope*. You will recall that a tightrope walker carries a long pole that extends for several feel horizontally on either side. By moving the pole up or down, the walker helps to maintain balance on the rope. Metaphorically, we can think of the horizontal pole as the body of knowledge that we build to help us recognize when we might lean too far to either side.

Balance allows us to integrate the concepts of actualization and differentiation; we learn how to be real and interdependent. We care for ourselves and for others. We strive for and achieve excellence. Our model is one of win-win rather than a competitive model that is built on winning at the expense of others. Achieving balance requires more than an intellectual knowledge.

A busy physician found himself in an emergency room—on a stretcher, with personnel scurrying about and hovering over him. He had collapsed in the parking lot of the hospital on his way to perform yet another surgery. Overwork, loss of sleep, rainy weather that encouraged him to skip regular exercise, fast food—all had contributed to imbalance. Now he was paying the price.

Developing equipoise need not equate with boredom. Our universe is anything but boring. The restless tides ebb and flow. The seasons come and go. The bow follows the rain. Every day has its darkness and its light. Similarly, human life has a natural rhythm. It includes highs and lows, joys and sorrows, pains and pleasures, work and play. Equipoise means that we can accept this rhythm with its endless variations. Without a sense of balance, we may be at risk for trying to smooth out the cadence of life into a straight line or to achieve a never-ending series of highs.

A sense of balanced discernment enables us to experience life's natural rhythms without aberrant swings. It allows us to experience living in all its vibrant fullness with its routines and variety, its gladness and sadness, its grief and ecstasy, its frustration and contentment—realizing that the rhythm of life will bring about its own change in its own time.

We ride the waves in our ship of life; neither falling overboard nor being swamped. Sometimes the waves are higher than usual; sometimes the waters are completely calm. Come what may, the ride will usually be more rewarding from a position of equipoise.

At times when we are experiencing frustration, it can be helpful to take a deep breath, step back, and *observe* ourselves against the backdrop of the moment. We can also ask ourselves the question, "In two years, how much importance will this moment still hold?" Such an exercise can help us to return more quickly to a position of balance.

Equipoise is to high-level-wellness living,
What emancipation is to freedom from slavery.

Equipoise—Day Two

Table Twenty-four—Problems with equipoise   Females—216 Males—102

	Never	Rarely	Sometimes	Frequently	Always
Females	6.5%	26.9%	45.8%	16.6%	4.2%
Males	10.8%	27.5%	39.2%	16.6%	5.8%
Overall	8.0%	27.0%	43.7%	16.6%	4.7%
Me					

Take a few moments to evaluate yourself:

- Are the physical, emotional, mental, spiritual, and sexual components of my life in balance?
- Does my life compare to a *yo-yo*?
- Is my life compulsively spinning out of balance?
- Am I able to maintain an inner calm regardless of the storms around me?
- Do minor annoyances upset my equilibrium?
- Are there problems in my life related to achieving a sense of balance?

Equipoise—Day Three

In all these things we are more than conquerors. Romans 8:37

I am making a list of the events in my life that have contributed to my ability to exhibit balance. Likewise I am listing the factors that influenced me to develop problems in the area of balance. I look at these events and factors from a new perspective and I am learning from them. I make a determined effort to give up the negative and to consistently practice the positive. Today I recognize the value of humor in the process of developing balance. When the pendulum swings too wide, I know that it will come back to the middle—that is the law of the pendulum. As I grow, the pendulum still swings but its swings are less erratic. However the pendulum swings, I can find something to laugh about. I know that I am a conqueror. Therefore, I can smile.

Equipoise—Day Four

...Remember that meditation is in reality intensely practical. One of its first fruits is emotional balance. Bill Wilson

When I don't always get everything I want, I remember that I have been spared some of the calamities that seem to *dog* those who have everything they desire in terms of material goods. I would rather not change places with them. However, I wouldn't be surprised if they have noticed my emerging equipoise. Today I ponder the internal voice that helps to guide me on my journey, that supports my sense of value, that encourages my character development, that cheers me through the needed improvements, that rejoices with me in lessons learned through inevitable mistakes, that encourages me to take the next step. Even as I enjoy the company of others, I realize that I have become my own best friend. Therefore, I do not fear being alone with myself—I even welcome it at times. I have learned that loneliness is just a state of mind. In addition, I always have my Higher Power. What comforting thoughts! Time for meditation sounds great!

Equipoise—Day Five

Nothing boomerangs faster than an unbalanced existence. Old Adage

I believe that I can learn balance through many of the situations and circumstances that I encounter. Some of the situations resemble sandpaper, others silk. I look for the lesson in the sandpaper and in the silk. I am content. My Higher Power watches over me and sees that I am choosing to do the very best I can at my present stage of development. Today I did a little better than I did yesterday. Tomorrow I will do a little better than I did today. I am making slow but steady progress. Balance in my life creates balance in my world. My words and actions are congruent; this entity stands undivided. I give myself the gift of caution, anyway. Because of that, in any given situation I am more likely to choose a balanced course of action. Equipoise is becoming my favorite cup of tea. I certainly waste a lot less adrenalin!

Equipoise—Day Six

*In this frenetic world of ours, achieving
balance is an art form all its own. Cherney*

I treat myself as if I am a treasure of inestimable value. Because I do this consistently, it is becoming a habit. Today I realize that this journey is very much like reading a good book; the farther I get into the text—*The Personal History of Me*—the more it begins to make sense. I do not expect to finish the book in one sitting; I may never finish it. Each day I read a few more pages and who I am is becoming clearer. Each page, each paragraph brings me another step closer to knowing who I really am; to believing in myself and my personal value. I compare equipoise to a checking account. I know that there can be no withdrawals unless I have made some deposits—whether or not I have two pads of checks left! Living in balance helps me to make deposits into my bank of life.

Equipoise—Day Seven

*Balance began in the heart of God and is
complete only when it reaches ours. Unknown*

Today I realize that it is okay to feel and to express satisfaction with myself and my accomplishments. I *pat myself on the back*. I thank myself for a job well done. As I learn to validate myself, I in turn validate others for their good work. I am becoming the person I was intended to be. I hold my head high. The puzzle pieces are coming together. I am so glad I embarked on this journey. Nothing will ever be the same again. I am carefully listening to my internal self-talk tapes about equipoise. I am rehearsing thoughts and words that help me to achieve and maintain equipoise; that help me to avoid the extremes of instability. My heart is being reached. There is now balance in my universe.

Equipoise—Day Eight

God grant me the serenity to accept the things
I cannot change, the courage to change the things
I can, and the wisdom to know the difference. Serenity Prayer

Life is a process, not a goal; a journey rather than a destination. As I truly understand this concept, life just gets better and better—more stable, more productive, and more enjoyable as I continue on the path of recovery. Today I see more improvement in attaining balance. I envision new opportunities, discover new ideas, learn new behaviors. I am content with who I am today; I am discontented with the idea of stagnation. Each open door beckons me toward another adventure. I enjoy exploring. I do not hold myself back from taking necessary risks nor do I fret about things I cannot change, for I have received the gifts of wisdom and serenity. Conversations with my Higher Power lately are mostly about gratitude!

Identify one specific behavior, in relation to equipoise, that you are striving to upgrade.

_____

_____

_____

_____

_____

Equipoise—Day Nine

List three facts you have learned about yourself in relation to achieving balance.

- _____

_____

- _____

_____

- _____

_____

Equipoise—Day Ten

Give yourself credit for the progress you are making in developing the power of maintaining equipoise. Write down your personal affirmation related to balance.

_____

_____

_____

_____

_____

_____

THE TWELVE STEPS OF REPARENTING

© Arlene Taylor PhD

STEP 1. I recognize that I have not completed all the developmental tasks of childhood and admit that in my own strength I am powerless to reparent myself successfully.

STEP 2. I believe that a Power greater than myself can restore me to wholeness and enable me to effectively reparent myself.

STEP 3. In this reparenting process, I make a decision to turn my will and my life over to the care of God, as I understand my Higher Power.

STEP 4. I am making a searching and fearless moral inventory of myself, doing family-of-origin work to discover the factors that interfered with the satisfactory completion of some of the development tasks of childhood.

STEP 5. I admit to my Higher Power, to myself, and to another human being the exact nature of the areas in which I need reparenting and am ready to have my Higher Power assist me in this process.

STEP 6. I am entirely ready to have my Higher Power help me to reparent myself and to complete the developmental tasks of childhood that I have not successfully learned.

STEP 7. I humbly ask God to remove my shortcomings and to give me clarity of vision in the reparenting process.

STEP 8. I am making a list of individuals I have harmed because of my immaturity, contributed to by unsatisfactory completion of some of the developmental tasks of childhood, and am willing to make amends.

STEP 9. Wherever and whenever possible, I am making amends to people I have harmed, except when to do so would injure them or others.

STEP 10. I continue to take personal inventory during my reparenting process and promptly admit when I am wrong.

STEP 11. I seek through prayer and meditation to improve my conscious contact with my Higher Power, asking for wisdom and energy to reparent myself toward wholeness.

STEP 12. I am reparenting myself toward wholeness and am sharing my experience with others as appropriate, encouraging them in their recovery and reparenting process even as I practice these principles in my life on a daily basis.

None of us reach adulthood without experiencing some dysfunction and loss because none of us had an entirely functional family system or role-models who were completely actualized and differentiated. Our parents (or parental figures) undoubtedly did the best they could at the time; most people do. This means that in general, all of us have some area(s) in which we can make improvements and move on to maturity.

Working through these twenty-four developmental tasks can be a giant step in figuring out who we are and in designing a more functional future for ourselves. Learning how to affirm ourselves and others can be another giant step. Breaking the cycle of dysfunction starts with us, individually. It begins with taking personal responsibility for ourselves and our present condition. It requires the hard work of recovery and healing—as well as the process of learning to exhibit healthier behaviors on a consistent basis. We call this process reparenting.

Some individuals were blessed with better role-models than were others. Those who were fortunate enough to have excellent parental role-models simply continue the process of moving toward wholeness. Those who had no role-models, or whose role-models did not possess the skills necessary to parent effectively, need to reparent themselves.

Reparenting can be defined as the act of caring for oneself in the manner of a *genuine* parent. Reparenting includes a need to:

- Complete the developmental tasks of childhood and to maintain recovery
- Live an affirming life, nurturing the self and others
- Bring one's life into thriving balance
- Role-model high-level-wellness functional living.

Why reparent? Because we are all role-modeling whether or not we realize that. If we are not doing it consciously, we are exhibiting subconsciously absorbed attitudes, beliefs, and expectations from childhood. Reparenting may be the most unselfish legacy we can give to the next generation. In reality, the best gift we can give to our children and to others is to take care of ourselves, to take care of our issues, to heal our woundedness, and to become actualized differentiated adults who can role-model desirable behaviors.

A teenager recently asked, "What is an adult, anyway?" That can be a difficult question to answer. Here is a beginning. An adult is an individual who:

- Has left home
- Has given up the need to be continually *parented* by someone else
- Theoretically at least, is capable of becoming a parent to someone else.

To *leave home* means to:

- Accept physical, emotional, intellectual, financial, sexual, and social responsibility for one's own life and destiny
- Give up dependency and fusion with parental figures and to avoid transferring those qualities to a spouse or partner
- To no longer be automatically programmed by the transgenerational script.

Reparenting helps us to write our own script; one that fits and maximizes our individual uniqueness. In a practical sense, when we write and follow our own script we:

- No longer feel compelled to work upon the unresolved problems or indiscretions of the previous generations
- Don't carry within us the toxic burden of unmourned loss and grief carried over from experiences of the previous generations
- Aren't obligated to ritualize in our own lives the beliefs, customs, and expectations of our ancestors

- Aren't immobilized either by the lack of validation or the conditional praise/love of the previous generations
- Aren't controlled by the need to make restitution for past generational failures or unfulfilled longings
- Have given up the need to confront, chastise, get rid of, demand from, or require generational ancestors to be different—accepting them exactly as they are
- Are able to value and respect previous generations simply for the position they hold in our generational inheritance
- Free ourselves to become the persons we were intended to be, utilizing our innate giftedness.

According to research data from The Developmental Task Survey, it is important for each of us to look at our own lives. It is highly likely we will need reparenting in at least one area. Through this learning process, we can make the world a better place than we found it.

RESEARCH DATA

The Developmental Task Survey—Selected demographic data.

PERCENTAGE OF QUESTIONNAIRES RETURNED

	# Distributed	# Returned	% Return
Females	300	232	77.3%
Males	300	103	34.3%
Overall	600	335	55.8%

AGE OF PARTICIPANTS

Answering this question: Females = 219   Males = 10

	<30	30-40	40-50	50-60	60-70	>70
Females	11.0%	20.5%	32.0%	16.0%	13.2%	7.3%
Males	6.0%	26.7%	25.7%	22.8%	11.9%	6.9%
Overall	9.4%	22.5%	30.0%	18.1%	12.8%	7.2%

BIRTH ORDER

Answering this question: Females = 217   Males = 101

	Only child	Oldest child	Oldest of gender	Youngest Child	Middle Child
Females	9.2%	31.3%	6.5%	30.0%	23.0%
Males	7.9%	32.7%	8.9%	25.7%	24.8%
Overall	8.8%	31.8%	7.2%	28.6%	23.6%

ETHNIC BACKGROUND

Answering this question: Females = 218   Males = 101

	Asian	Black	Caucasian	Hispanic	Other
Females	0.9%	1.8%	93.2%	4.1%	0.0%
Males	0.0%	1.0%	95.0%	2.0%	2.0%
Overall	0.6%	1.6%	93.7%	3.5%	0.6%

TYPE OF GRADE SCHOOLS PRIMARILY ATTENDED

Answering this question: Female = 218   Male = 101

	Public schools	Parochial schools
Females	56.9%	43.1%
Males	64.4%	35.6%
Overall	59.2%	40.8%

TYPE OF HIGH SCHOOLS PRIMARILY ATTENDED
Answering this question: Female = 218   Male = 101

	Public schools	Parochial schools	Home study
Females	52.1%	47.5%	0.4%
Males	55.0%	45.0%	0%
Overall	53.0%	46.7%	0.3%

TYPE OF COLLEGES/UNIVERSITIES PRIMARILY ATTENDED
Answering this question: Female = 218   Male = 101

	Public	Parochial	Other/private
Females	42.9%	48.8%	8.3%
Males	39.6%	43.8%	16.6%
Overall	41.9%	47.2%	10.9%

CAREER OR OCCUPATION
Answering this question: Females = 219   Males = 100

	Construction	Health-related	Education	Business/banking	Public Service	Other
Females	17.8%	40.0%	20.5%	5.5%	19.2%	0.0%
Males	15.0%	19.0%	14.0%	7.0%	9.0%	36.0%
Overall	17.0%	28.2%	18.5%	6.0%	16.0%	11.3%

MOST RECENT SALARY RATE/RANGE
Answering this question: Females = 201   Males = 94

	<$10 per hour	$10-$20 per hour	$20-$30 per hour	>$30 per hour
Females	31.3%	41.8%	18.9%	8.0%
Males	10.6%	51.1%	23.4%	14.9%
Overall	24.8%	44.8%	20.3%	10.1%

MARITAL STATUS
Answering this question: Females = 219   Males = 101

	Single - Never married	Married	Separated	Single - Divorced	Re-married	Widow/widower
Females	12.8%	60.5%	2.3%	15.5%	6.4%	2.3%
Males	11.0%	72.0%	4.0%	3.0%	10.0%	1.0%
Overall	12.2%	64.3%	2.8%	11.5%	7.5%	1.7%

PERCENTAGE WHO HAVE CHILDREN
Answering this question: Females = 219   Males = 101

	No child(ren)	No biological child(ren)	Have biological child(ren)	Have step-child(ren)	Have foster child(ren)	Have adopted child(ren)
Females	21.5%	1.4%	71.75	3.2%	0.4%	1.8%
Males	17.8%	1.0%	77.2%	1.0%	1.0%	2.0%
Overall	20.4%	1.3%	70.4%	2.5%	0.6%	3.8%

PERCENTAGE OF TIME SPENT AT CAREER/OCCUPATION
Answering this question: Females = 213   Males = 99

	Work full time	Work part time	Retired/volunteer/ or none
Females	57.7%	23.5%	18.8%
Males	79.8%	6.1%	14.1%
Overall	64.7%	18.0%	17.3%

ATTEND RELIGIOUS SERVICES
Answering this questions: Females = 219   Males = 101

	Regularly	Frequently	Rarely	Never
Females	66.2%	12.3%	15.1%	6.4%
Males	68.3%	12.9%	14.9%	3.9%
Overall	66.9%	12.5%	15.0%	5.6%

SATISFIED WITH GENDER
Answering this question: Females = 219   Males = 101

	Glad to be a female	Wished had been born male	Never thought about it	Wished male opportunities	Other (write in)
Females	31.1%	14.1%	30.6%	22.4%	1.8%
Gender	Glad to be a male	Wished had been born female	Never thought about it		Other (write in)
Males	46.6%	4.9%	45.6%		2.9%

EDUCATIONAL BACKGROUND
Answering this question: Females = 216   Males = 100

	Only High School	Some college	AS/AA only	BS/BA only	MA/MS only	PhD/ MD
Females	7.8%	29.6%	11.1%	31.1%	15.3%	5.1%
Males	11.0%	26.0%	9.0%	26.0%	24.0%	4.0%
Overall	8.9%	28.5%	10.4%	29.4%	18.1%	4.7%

HISTORY OF EXPERIENCING GENDER DISCRIMINATION
Answering this question: Females = 214   Males = 100

	None	Major	Some
Females	33.2%	20.1%	46.7%
Males	80.0%	7.0%	13.0%
Overall	48.1%	15.9%	36.0%

UNDERSTAND CONCEPT OF REPARENTING ONESELF
Answering this question: Females = 219   Males = 98

	Understand reparenting	Do not understand
Females	50.7%	49.3%
Males	36.7%	63.3%
Overall	46.4%	53.6%

ENGAGED IN THE PROCESS OF REPARENTING
\# Answering this question: Females = 219   Males = 99

	Engaged in reparenting	Not engaged in reparenting
Females	33.3%	66.7%
Males	23.2%	76.8%
Overall	30.2%	69.8%

HISTORY OF EXPERIENCING MENTAL ABUSE
\# Answering this question: Females = 217   Males = 97

	Have experienced mental abuse	No mental abuse experienced
Females	41.9%	58.1%
Males	32.0%	68.0%
Overall	38.9%	61.1%

HISTORY OF EXPERIENCING EMOTIONAL ABUSE
\# Answering this question: Females = 219   Males = 100

	Have experienced emotional abuse	No emotional abuse experienced
Females	63.0%	37.0%
Males	44.0%	56.0%
Overall	57.1%	42.9%

HISTORY OF EXPERIENCING PHYSICAL ABUSE
\# Answering this question: Females = 219   Males = 98

	Have experienced physical abuse	No physical abuse experienced
Females	30.6%	69.4%
Males	24.5%	75.5%
Overall	28.7%	71.3%

HISTORY OF EXPERIENCING SPIRITUAL ABUSE
\# Answering this question: Females = 218   Males = 97

	Have experienced spiritual abuse	No spiritual abuse experienced
Females	21.1%	78.9%
Males	14.4%	85.6%
Overall	19.0%	81.0%

HISTORY OF EXPERIENCING SEXUAL ABUSE
\# Answering this question: Females = 219   Males = 98

	Have experienced sexual abuse	No sexual abuse experienced
Females	29.7%	70.3%
Males	11.2%	88.8%
Overall	23.9%	76.1%

HISTORY OF EXPERIENCING "OTHER" TYPES OF ABUSE
Answering this question: Females = 218   Males = 97

	Have experienced	Have not experienced
Females	5.5%	97.9%
Males	2.1%	97.9%
Overall	4.4%	95.6%

ALCOHOLISM PRESENT IN FAMILY-OF-ORIGIN
Answering this question: Females = 219   Males = 100

	Alcoholism present	No alcoholism
Females	29.2%	70.8%
Males	23.0%	77.0%
Overall	27.2%	72.7%

OTHER DRUG MISUSE PRESENT IN FAMILY-OF-ORIGIN
Answering this question: Females = 218   Males = 98

	Yes	No
Females	8.7%	91.3%
Males	6.1%	93.9%
Overall	7.9%	92.1%

OTHER ADDICTIONS PRESENT IN FAMILY-OF-ORIGIN
(e.g., sex, illness, control, religion, anger)
Answering this question: Females = 218   Males = 98

	Yes	No
Females	39.9%	60.1%
Males	29.6%	70.4%
Overall	36.7%	63.3%

ABUSIVE PATTERNS OF BEHAVIOR IN FAMILY-OF-ORIGIN
Answering this question: Females = 218   Males = 97

	Yes	No
Females	32.1%	67.9%
Males	24.7%	75.3%
Overall	29.8%	70.2%

UNWED PREGNANCY IN FAMILY-OF-ORIGIN
Answering this question: Females = 218   Males = 98

	Yes	No
Females	15.1%	84.9%
Males	8.2%	91.8%
Overall	12.9%	87.1%

OTHER DYSFUNCTION IN FAMILY-OF-ORIGIN
Answering this question: Females = 218   Males = 97

	Yes	No
Females	8.7%	91.3%
Males	9.3%	90.7%
Overall	8.9%	91.1%

IN PROCESS OF RECOVERING FROM CODEPENDENCY
Answering this question: Females = 218   Males = 97

	Yes	No
Females	32.6%	83.5%
Males	16.5%	83.5%
Overall	27.6%	72.4%

IN PROCESS OF RECOVERING FROM SOME TYPE OF ADDICTION
Answering this question: Females = 218   Males = 98

	Yes	No
Females	11.9%	88.1%
Males	19.4%	80.6%
Overall	14.2%	85.8%

RECOVERING FROM A DYSFUNCTIONAL CHILDHOOD
Answering this question: Females = 219   Males = 99

	Yes	No
Females	36.1%	63.9%
Males	18.2%	81.8%
Overall	30.5%	69.5%

RECOVERING FROM AN ABUSIVE RELATIONSHIP
Answering this question: Females = 218   Males = 97

	Yes	No
Females	20.6%	79.4%
Males	4.15	95.9%
Overall	15.5%	84.5%

RECOVERING FROM OTHER TYPE OF DYSFUNCTION
Answering this question: Females = 218   Males = 97

	Yes	No
Females	6.8%	93.2%
Males	7.2%	92.8%
Overall	6.9%	93.1%

POSTSCRIPT

Arlene Taylor is founder and president of Realizations Inc —an education, consulting, and brain-profiling service. In addition to her roles as author, speaker, and brain function consultant, she is also Director of Risk Management and Infection Control at an acute-care hospital.

Taylor is a Diplomate with the National Board of Christian Clinical Therapists. She mentors selected bachelor, masters, and doctoral students (primarily those with an interest in brain function). With the goal of helping others to enhance their personal and spiritual growth, she enjoys presenting *seminars of distinction* internationally as well as counseling individuals/couples in connection with their BTSA profiles. She and her husband make their home in the beautiful Napa Valley of Northern California.

Her educational background includes:

- A Doctorate in Clinical Counseling
- Licensure to administer, score, and interpret the Benziger Thinking Styles Assessment (BTSA)
- A Doctorate in Health & Human Services
- A Master of Science in Epidemiology and Health Education
- A Bachelor of Science in Nursing
- A Public Health Nursing certificate and a Health & Development credential, State of California.

Lorna Lawrence is an author, educational consultant, peer counselor, musician, and world traveler. She has presented musical and variety concerts internationally. She also enjoys conducting seminars on personal growth.

She has taught school and/or has been a principal in several countries including the United States, Canada, Japan, and the Philippines. The experience of dealing with inter-cultural children and their families has given her an enriched firsthand perspective.

Lawrence believes that families, regardless of their cultural backgrounds, have similar needs and exhibit similar parenting problems in relation to the developmental tasks of childhood. Special interests include counseling in the areas of personal growth, family-of-origin work, temperament types, crisis intervention, sexual abuse, incest survival, and recovery/reparenting issues.

Lorna makes her home in the Sacramento Valley of Northern California where she teaches grades three and four, directs the Lorna Lawrence Women's Ensemble, conducts support groups, and offers counseling based on the N.C.C.A.'s Temperament Analysis Profile (T.A.P.).

Her educational background includes:

- A Doctorate in Clinical Counseling
- A Master of Education (with an emphasis in *blended families*)
- A Bachelor of Science in Elementary Education.

Debby Wilmot is a musician, author, minister's wife, and registered nurse with a Bachelor of Science Degree. She has taught piano part time and enjoys composing music for voice, keyboard, and guitar. Instruments on which Debby performs proficiently include the piano, organ, guitar, French horn, and trumpet. She has been associated with a variety of musical groups as singer and/or accompanist and has cut a record with Maranatha Singers. Several times she has been commissioned to write theme songs for women's groups.

Debby also enjoys hiking, body building, playing on a softball team, and acrylic painting (some of her paintings have been exhibited). Her interest in line-drawing resulted in her being invited to create a set of illustrations, each designed to depict a developmental task. Currently she lives with her husband and two teenage sons in Northern California.

SELECTED BIBLIOGRAPHY

Benziger, I. Katherine. *THE ART OF USING YOUR WHOLE BRAIN* (KBA Publishing:TX)

Bradshaw, John. *HOME COMING* (Bantam Books:NY)

Brandon, Nathaniel. *HOW TO RAISE YOUR SELF-ESTEEM* (Bantam Books:NY)

Buhler, Rich. *NEW CHOICES. NEW BOUNDARIES* (Thomas Nelson Publishers:TN)

Cloud, Henry and Townsend, John. *BOUNDARIES* (Zondervan Publishing House:MI)

Dyer, Wayne. *YOUR ERRONEOUS ZONES* (Avon Books:NY)

Emery, Stewart with Rogin, Neal. *ACTUALIZATIONS-You Don't Have to Rehearse to Be Yourself* (Doubleday & Company, Inc:NY)

Erikson, Erik H. *CHILDHOOD AND SOCIETY.* (W.W.Norton & Company, Inc:NY)

Forward, Susan. *TOXIC PARENTS.* (Bantam Books:NY)

Helmstetter, Shad. *WHAT TO SAY WHEN YOU TALK TO YOURSELF* (Pocket Books:NY)

McCarthy, Kevin, W. *THE ON-PURPOSE PERSON. A Modern Parable.* (Pinon Press:CO)

Middleton-Moz, Jane and Dwinell, Lorie. *AFTER THE TEARS* (Health Communications Inc:FL)

Missildine, W. Hugh. *YOUR INNER CHILD OF THE PAST* (Simon & Schuster:NY)

Pollard, John K. III. *SELF-PARENTING* (Generic Human Studies Publishing:CA)

Smalley, Gary and Trent, John. *THE BLESSING* (Pocket Books, Simon & Schuster:NY)

Taylor, Arlene. *BACK TO BASICS* (Teach Services Inc:NY)

Viscott, David. *THE LANGUAGE OF FEELINGS* (Pocket Books, Simon & Schuster:NY)

Weber, Martin. *HURT, HEALING & HAPPY AGAIN* (Review & Herald Publishing Association:MD)

RESOURCES

The following are examples of resources available from:

Realizations Inc
PO Box 2554
Napa CA 94558-0255
707•554•4981

BACK TO BASICS. $10. Dr. Taylor combines strategies for building Optimum Self-Esteem and Bona Fide Boundaries in her recent 247 page illustrated paperback. It is about real people and their real-life experiences. Every man, woman, and child stands to benefit from these succinct prevention and recovery strategies.

Timely and clearly written— M.F.C.C., California	A rich motherlode of information— Family physician, Canada
A truly valuable guide— Teacher, Michigan	A jewel of a self-help book—Counselor, Guam

THE BENZIGER THINKING STYLES ASSESSMENT (BTSA). Dr. Taylor is licensed to administer, score, and interpret the BTSA. This twenty-page personalized interpretation can enhance your ability to understand, appreciate, and maximize your uniqueness. The BTSA profiles thinking style, *brain lead,* risk for excessive adaption/burnout/mid-life crisis, career match, emotional tone, extroversion/introversion level. It can be completed by mail at your pace. The price of $125 is less than the cost of two hours of professional counseling in most areas. This could very well be the most valuable gift you ever give yourself! Couples also receive a *couple's analysis.*

Write or call for a complete listing of available resources.
Visa/Master Card accepted.